INSTANT
ONE-POT
MEALS

INSTANT
ONE-POT
MEALS

SOUTHERN RECIPES FOR THE MODERN 7-IN-1 ELECTRIC PRESSURE COOKER

LAURA ARNOLD

THE COUNTRYMAN PRESS
A division of W. W. Norton & Company
Independent Publishers Since 1923

FOR MY DAD,

THANKS FOR ALL OF
YOUR LOVE AND SUPPORT IN
MY FOODIE ADVENTURES

CONTENTS

INTRODUCTION

★ ★ ★

Cooking Southern food can often seem daunting. Classic recipes call for so many ingredients, and it can take hours of love to turn out the end result. *Instant One-Pot Meals* takes traditional Southern recipes and adapts them, using the electric pressure cooker—now all of that Southern flavor can be made in around an hour or less, so you don't have to labor over the stove for an entire afternoon. Just imagine being able to get Southern Barbecue Ribs or Collard Greens with Bacon on the table after a long day at the workplace! And it gets even better: try making Hummingbird Cake or Key Lime Pie for dessert and say good-bye to packaged ice cream and cookies as an after-dinner sweet treat.

In addition, nearly all the recipes in this book are one-pot dishes, meaning that you can cook these recipes in minimal time, and you only have one pot to clean. And don't think you can only use your electric pressure cooker for dinner and dessert—you can also use it to make breakfast, sides, condiments, and stocks in minimal time. Whether you're cooking dinner after a long day of work or entertaining on the fly, *Instant One-Pot Meals* provides you with simple, easy solutions to get delicious Southern cooking on the table in no time.

USING YOUR ELECTRIC PRESSURE COOKER

Most modern electric pressure cookers have at least 7 functions: Pressure, Sauté, Slow Cook, Rice Cook, Steam, Yogurt, and Keep Warm. The recipes in this book mainly use the Manual pressure cooker setting, with variations for the Slow Cook setting for certain recipes. The Manual setting allows you to adjust the amount of pressure between high pressure and low pressure so that a complex dish turns out perfect every time.

When using your pressure cooker it is important to refer to the user manual for your specific model. Basic use of the pressure cooker first involves locking the lid and listening for the beeping noise to ensure it is secure. Second, be sure the steam valve is in the locked position on top of the pressure cooker. Choose the Manual setting or another setting appropriately and select high pressure or low pressure and a time period. The pressure cooker will take anywhere from 5 to 10 minutes to come to pressure. This adds additional cooking time, but the benefit is that you do not need to watch the pot once cooking has begun.

When the pressure cooker is finished cooking it will beep, signaling you to completely shut off the pressure cooker or to select the Keep Warm setting until you are ready to serve. It is best to shut off the pressure cooker so that the contents inside do not overcook. When you are ready to open the pressure cooker, you have a choice of either a quick release of pressure or a natural release of pressure. Quick release involves opening the valve to immediately release all of the steam. *Be sure to release the steam with the valve facing away from you!* To reduce the amount of steam coming out of the pressure cooker, use a towel to cover the valve when using either quick release or natural release. Using natural release allows the pressure cooker to release the steam slowly on its own. Natural release is performed by turning the machine off and waiting for the float steam valve to drop naturally (refer to your pressure cooker manual for image). Natural release can take up to 15 minutes. Several recipes in this book call for natural release for 10 minutes and then a quick release to speed the process, allowing you to get dinner on the table faster. Once the dish is finished cooking, the liquid in the pot often needs to be reduced and thickened. This is very easy to do in the pressure cooker—just set the pot to the Sauté setting and allow the liquid to simmer until it has thickened appropriately.

Whenever you are removing the lid of the pressure cooker, be sure to open the lid facing away from you. Doing so prevents you from coming into contact with excess hot steam that might be in the vessel.

When making cakes or other recipes that use a cake pan, it is helpful to make a foil strap that wraps around the bottom of the cake pan. This foil strap will serve as handles when you lower and lift the pan into the pressure cooker. Use a piece of foil that is about 20 inches in length, and then fold the foil until you form a 1-inch-wide strap. Place the strap under the bottom of the cake pan, and then use the side lengths of the foil strap to lower and lift the pan into and out of the pressure cooker.

SPECIAL EQUIPMENT

Making bakes, casseroles, dips, and even desserts like cakes and cobblers require special baking pans that will fit inside of the pressure cooker. The pans used in this book are:

- 6-inch round cake pan or soufflé dish (2 to 3 inches deep)
- 7-inch round cake pan or soufflé dish (2 to 3 inches deep)
- 8-inch springform pan
- Two (5½-by-3-inch) mini loaf pans (optional)

Many of the recipes in this book use a broiler to finish the dish. Use the broiler where indicated for a toasted, crunchy top for casseroles and bakes or to crisp the skin on chicken dishes. When listed as optional, you can skip this step for quicker cooking or to avoid using multiple appliances.

BREAKFAST

* * *

★ ★ ★

BANANAS FOSTER FRENCH TOAST

★ ★ ★

This is the perfect recipe for French toast without the hassle! With this easy recipe, there's no need to dip each piece of bread in egg and cook 1 or 2 pieces at a time. Just mix together the ingredients and let the pressure cooker do the work.

1½ cups water

Cooking spray, for pan

½ cup whole milk

3 eggs, lightly beaten

1 teaspoon vanilla extract

½ teaspoon cinnamon

¼ teaspoon allspice

¼ cup brown sugar

½ cup sugar

½ teaspoon kosher salt

3¼ cups day-old sourdough or white bread, cut into ½-inch cubes

½ cup pecans, roughly chopped

2 bananas, peeled and sliced

Maple syrup, warmed, to serve

SERVES 4

PREP TIME: 15 minutes
COOK TIME: 20 minutes

SLOW COOKER SETTING

Follow the steps below. In step 2, select Slow Cook then place on the normal setting and cook for 1½ to 2 hours, or until the eggs are cooked through.

1 Place the steam rack inside the electric pressure cooker and add the water to the bottom of the pot. Grease a 6- to 7-inch soufflé dish or 6-inch round cake pan with cooking spray.

2 Add the milk, eggs, vanilla extract, cinnamon, allspice, brown sugar, sugar, and salt to a large bowl and mix to combine. Add the bread, pecans, and bananas and push down to soak the bread for 5 to 10 minutes. Pour the soaked bread mixture into the baking dish and press down. Place a paper towel and then a piece of foil on top of the baking dish. Place the dish inside of the pressure cooker on top of the steam rack. Secure the lid and cook on Manual with high pressure for 10 minutes. Allow to naturally release for 5 minutes, then quick release and remove the lid.

3 For toasted edges, if desired, preheat the broiler and place the baking dish under the broiler to toast the bread on top, 4 to 5 minutes. Remove from the broiler and serve with maple syrup.

CHEESE GRITS
WITH TOMATO GRAVY

★ ★ ★

The flavor of cheddar with tomato is a Southern classic.
Try adding bacon for a twist!

SERVES 4 TO 6

PREP TIME: 10 minutes
COOK TIME: 25 minutes

SLOW COOKER
SETTING

Combine the ingredients for the grits in the bowl of the slow cooker, adding an additional 1 cup of water. Cook on the Slow Cook low setting for 6 to 7 hours. Add the ingredients for the tomato gravy and select the Slow Cook low setting for an additional hour, and then serve.

FOR THE TOMATO GRAVY

1 tablespoon olive oil

½ onion, finely chopped

1 (15-ounce) can whole peeled tomatoes

1 teaspoon fresh thyme leaves or 2 teaspoons dried thyme

1 teaspoon kosher salt

½ teaspoon freshly ground black pepper

2 tablespoons flour

FOR THE GRITS

1 cup stone-ground grits or cornmeal

1½ cups water

1 cup whole milk

1 teaspoon kosher salt

½ teaspoon freshly ground black pepper

2 tablespoons unsalted butter, diced

1¼ cups shredded sharp Cheddar, divided

1 **MAKE THE TOMATO GRAVY** Heat the oil in the electric pressure cooker on the Sauté setting. Add the onion and cook until softened, about 4 minutes. Add the tomatoes and cook, breaking up with the back of a wooden spoon. Bring to a simmer and allow the liquid to reduce slightly. Add the thyme, salt, and pepper. Add the flour and whisk to combine. Bring to a simmer and allow to thicken, about 3 minutes.

2 **MAKE THE CHEESE GRITS** Combine all the ingredients except the cheese. Pour over the tomatoes, secure the pressure cooker lid and cook on Manual with low pressure for 10 minutes.

3 Allow the pressure cooker to naturally release, then stir in 1 cup of the cheese.

4 Divide among bowls and garnish with the remaining ¼ cup of cheese.

SAUSAGE, EGG, AND CHEESE STRATA

★ ★ ★

SERVES 4
PREP TIME: 15 minutes
COOK TIME: 35 minutes

In this strata, three breakfast classics come together in a delicious bake that is perfect for entertaining on the fly. Swap out the sausage for bacon or your favorite vegetables to create countless variations.

1 tablespoon olive oil

½ pound loose breakfast sausage

½ red onion, finely diced

1½ cups water

1 tablespoon unsalted butter, for greasing pan

4 large eggs

¾ cup whole milk

½ teaspoon paprika

1 teaspoon fresh thyme or 2 teaspoons dried thyme

1 teaspoon kosher salt

½ teaspoon freshly ground black pepper

3 cups day-old sourdough, white, or wheat bread, cut in 1-inch cubes

1 cup shredded Cheddar, divided

Parsley, to garnish (optional)

1. Heat the olive oil in a large sauté pan over medium-high heat. Add the sausage and cook, breaking up with the back of a wooden spoon until crumbled and browned, about 7 minutes. Add the onion and cook until almost softened, about 4 minutes. Remove from heat and allow to cool slightly.

2. Place the steam rack in the bottom of the electric pressure cooker and pour in the water. Grease a 6-inch round cake pan or soufflé dish with butter.

3. Combine the eggs, milk, paprika, thyme, salt, and pepper and whisk to combine in a large bowl. Add the sausage mixture, bread cubes, and ¾ cup of the cheese and mix to combine.

4. Cover the pan with a paper towel and foil and press down. Place in the pressure cooker and secure the lid. Cook on

Manual with high pressure for 10 minutes. Allow to naturally release for 10 minutes, then quick release and remove the lid. Remove the baking dish from the pressure cooker and top with the remaining ¼ cup of cheese.

5 Preheat the broiler. Place the cake pan underneath the broiler until the cheese is melted and golden brown, 4 to 5 minutes. Garnish with parsley, if you prefer.

BANANA BREAD

★ ★ ★

SERVES 4 TO 6
PREP TIME: 15 minutes
COOK TIME: 1 hour

Banana Bread is perfect for breakfast, a snack, or even dessert! Make this delicious bread in advance and freeze for an easy weekday morning treat. Try adding chocolate chips to turn the banana bread into a dessert!

1½ cups water

1 stick plus 1 tablespoon unsalted butter, softened and divided

1¾ cups flour, divided

1 teaspoon baking soda

½ teaspoon kosher salt

¼ cup light brown sugar

¾ cup sugar

2 large eggs

3 ripe bananas, peeled and mashed

1 teaspoon vanilla extract

½ cup semi-sweet mini chocolate chips (optional)

1 Place the steam rack inside of the pressure cooker and add the water. Make a foil strap (see page 9) for the baking dish. Grease a 7-inch round cake pan with 1 tablespoon of the butter and dust with ¼ cup of the flour.

2 Whisk together the remaining 1½ cups flour, baking soda, and salt in a large bowl. Beat the remaining 1 stick butter and sugars together until light and fluffy in a second bowl with a hand-held mixer, or in the bowl of a stand mixer, about 4 minutes. Add the eggs, one at a time, beating after each addition until incorporated. Add the bananas and vanilla and beat until just combined. Add the flour mixture, a little at a time, and beat until just combined. Gently stir in the chocolate chips, if using.

3 Transfer to the baking dish and set in the pressure cooker. Place a paper towel and then a piece of foil on top of the baking dish. Secure the lid, set on Manual with high pressure for 50 minutes and natural release for 10 minutes or until an inserted

toothpick comes out clean. If necessary to cook longer, secure the lid back on the pressure cooker and select Manual with high pressure for an additional 5 minutes. Allow to naturally release for 5 minutes, then quick release and remove the lid. Remove from the pressure cooker and allow to cool completely in the pan.

CINNAMON STREUSEL COFFEE CAKE

★ ★ ★

SERVES 4 TO 6
PREP TIME: 25 minutes
COOK TIME: 65 minutes

Make the base of the cake in the electric pressure cooker in advance. Before serving, sprinkle with the streusel topping and pop the cake under the broiler. This will crisp the streusel and warm the cake through.

FOR THE STREUSEL

½ stick unsalted butter, chilled and cubed

¼ cup light brown sugar

½ cup flour

½ teaspoon kosher salt

½ teaspoon ground cinnamon

⅔ cup pecans, chopped

FOR THE CAKE

1½ cups water

Cooking spray, for greasing pan

1⅓ cups flour

1 teaspoon baking soda

½ teaspoon kosher salt

1 stick of unsalted butter, softened

¼ cup light brown sugar

½ cup granulated sugar

1 teaspoon vanilla extract

2 large eggs

¾ cup low-fat plain yogurt

1 **MAKE THE STREUSEL** Combine all the streusel ingredients in a small bowl. Work the butter into the mixture using your hands until pea-size pieces form. Refrigerate the streusel until ready to use.

2 **MAKE THE CAKE** Set the steam rack inside of the pressure cooker and add the water. Make a foil strap (see page 9) for a 7-inch round cake pan. Grease the cake pan with cooking spray.

continued

3 Whisk together the flour, baking soda, and salt in a large bowl. In a separate bowl, using a handheld mixer or in the bowl of a stand mixer, beat the butter and sugars together until light and fluffy, about 4 minutes. Add the vanilla extract and the eggs, one at a time, beating after each addition until incorporated. Add the yogurt and mix until just incorporated. Add the flour mixture, a little at a time, and mix until just combined.

4 Transfer half the batter to the cake pan, then sprinkle with two-thirds of the streusel. Add the remaining half of the batter on top. Cover with a paper towel and foil and place in the electric pressure cooker. Secure the lid and cook on Manual with high pressure for 50 minutes. Use natural release for 10 minutes, then use quick release and remove the lid. Remove the coffee cake from the electric pressure cooker and allow to cool in the pan for 10 minutes.

5 Before serving, preheat the broiler. Sprinkle the remaining streusel topping on top of the coffee cake and place under the broiler to cook until the butter has melted and topping is crisp, about 5 minutes. Remove, allow to cool slightly, and serve.

BACON, EGG, AND BISCUIT BAKE

★ ★ ★

Using leftover or store-bought biscuits is a simple solution to saving time when making this easy bake that is sure to be a crowd pleaser. Forget making biscuits, eggs, and bacon for brunch when you can make this easy dish.

SERVES 4

PREP TIME: 20 minutes
COOK TIME: 35 minutes

SLOW COOKER SETTING

Follow the directions below. For step 4, once the lid of the pressure cooker has been secured, select the Slow Cook normal setting and cook for 1½ to 2 hours or until the eggs are cooked through.

1 tablespoon olive oil

6 slices bacon

½ red onion, finely diced

1 green bell pepper, stemmed, seeded, and small diced

¼ teaspoon cayenne pepper

1 teaspoon kosher salt

½ teaspoon freshly ground black pepper

Cooking spray, to grease

4 large eggs

¾ cup low-fat milk

1 cup shredded Monterey Jack, divided

3 cups store-bought or leftover biscuits, cut into ½-inch pieces (about 3½ biscuits total)

1½ cups water

Parsley, chopped, to garnish (optional)

1 Heat the olive oil in a large sauté pan over medium-high heat. Add the bacon and cook until crispy, about 7 minutes. Transfer to a paper towel–lined plate and crumble. Drain excess fat from pan. Add the onion and bell pepper and cook until softened, about 4 minutes. Add the cayenne pepper and season with salt and pepper. Remove from the heat and cool slightly.

2 Grease a 6-inch round cake pan or soufflé dish with cooking spray.

3 Whisk the eggs and milk in a large bowl. Add the bacon, onion mixture, ¾ cup of the cheese, and biscuits and toss to combine. Transfer to the cake pan and press the biscuits down, allowing to sit for 5 minutes. Cover with a paper towel and then a piece of foil.

4 Place the steam rack inside of the pressure cooker and add the water. Make a foil strap (see page 9) to go around the cake pan for easy removal. Place the cake pan inside the pressure cooker, secure the lid, and set on Manual with high pressure for 10 minutes. Allow to naturally release for 10 minutes, then quick release and remove the lid.

5 Preheat the broiler. Sprinkle the remaining ¼ cup cheese over the bake. Place the biscuit bake under the broiler to toast the top pieces of biscuits and to melt the cheese, 3 to 4 minutes. Garnish with parsley, if using.

SOFT BOILED EGGS
IN SPICY TOMATO SAUCE

★ ★ ★

Poaching eggs in tomato sauce, peppers, and zucchini takes an everyday meal to another level. Use whatever fresh vegetables are in season

2 tablespoons olive oil

½ red onion, finely diced

2 garlic cloves, minced

1 green bell pepper, stemmed, seeded, and small diced

1 medium zucchini, medium diced (about 2 cups)

1 teaspoon kosher salt

½ teaspoon freshly ground black pepper

1 teaspoon fresh thyme or 2 teaspoons dried thyme

1 teaspoon ground cumin

Pinch cayenne pepper

¼ teaspoon crushed red pepper flakes (optional)

1 (15-ounce) can crushed tomatoes

4 large eggs

¼ cup parsley, chopped, to garnish (optional)

Crumbled feta cheese, to garnish (optional)

4 pieces pita bread, warmed

SERVES 4

PREP TIME: 15 minutes
COOK TIME: 25 minutes

SLOW COOKER
SETTING

After step 1, below, secure the lid and select the Slow Cook normal setting for 1½ to 2 hours. When ready to cook the eggs, remove the lid and proceed with step 3.

1 Heat the oil in the pressure cooker on the Sauté setting. Once hot, add the onion, garlic, bell pepper, and zucchini and cook until the onion is translucent and zucchini is light golden, about 6 minutes. Season with salt and pepper and add the thyme, cumin, cayenne, and crushed red pepper flakes, if using. Add the tomatoes and bring to a simmer.

2 Secure the lid of the pressure cooker and place on Manual with low pressure for 10 minutes. Allow to naturally release for 5 minutes, then quick release and remove the lid.

3 Return to the Sauté setting and bring the sauce to a simmer. Drop the eggs in one by one, making pockets in the sauce, and simmer until the whites are just cooked through but the yolks are still runny, 3 to 4 minutes. Garnish with parsley and feta cheese, if using, and serve with pita bread.

LEMON BLUEBERRY OATMEAL

★ ★ ★

Forget sitting by the stove stirring your oats for 30 minutes in the morning. With this recipe your oatmeal is finished in 15 minutes, all while you go about getting ready for your day! For different flavors, try adding your favorite fruits, jams, and spices to your oats.

Cooking spray, to grease

1 cup steel-cut oats

2½ cups water

½ cup low-fat milk

1 teaspoon cinnamon

¼ teaspoon nutmeg

½ teaspoon vanilla extract

3 tablespoons dark brown sugar, plus additional to serve

Zest of 1 lemon

1 cup blueberries, to garnish

2 bananas, peeled and sliced, to garnish

SERVES 4

PREP TIME: 3 minutes
COOK TIME: 22 minutes

SLOW COOKER
SETTING

Add 1 cup of extra water in step 1. For step 2, secure the lid and select the Slow Cook low setting and cook for 6 to 7 hours.

1 Grease the bowl of the electric pressure cooker with cooking spray. Add the oats, water, milk, cinnamon, nutmeg, vanilla, brown sugar, and lemon zest and stir to combine.

2 Secure the lid and set on Manual with high pressure for 12 minutes. Allow the lid to naturally release for 10 minutes, then quick release and remove the lid.

3 Stir the oatmeal and divide between bowls. Garnish with blueberries, bananas, and extra brown sugar, if desired.

SAUSAGE GRAVY
WITH BISCUIT DUMPLINGS

★ ★ ★

SERVES 4
PREP TIME: 5 minutes
COOK TIME: 23 minutes

You probably never thought that sausage gravy and biscuits could be made in the same pot—let alone in a pressure cooker. This easy biscuit dumpling recipe allows you to create homemade biscuits in a quarter of the time it takes to make biscuits the traditional way. Why not treat yourself?

FOR THE GRAVY

1 tablespoon olive oil

1 (12-ounce) package loose pork sausage, hot or mild

3 tablespoons flour

1½ cups low-fat milk

½ teaspoon smoked paprika or paprika

1 teaspoon fresh thyme or 2 teaspoons dried thyme

1 teaspoon kosher salt

½ teaspoon freshly ground black pepper

FOR THE BISCUIT DUMPLINGS

¾ cup baking mix, such as Bisquick

⅓ cup low-fat milk

1 teaspoon freshly ground black pepper

1 teaspoon fresh thyme leaves or 2 teaspoons dried thyme leaves

1 MAKE THE GRAVY Heat the olive oil on the Sauté setting of the pressure cooker. Add the sausage and cook until browned, about 8 minutes. Add the flour and stir to coat the meat. Slowly add the milk and bring to a simmer, stirring to combine. Allow the milk to thicken slightly, about 4 minutes, and then add the paprika, thyme, salt, and pepper.

2 MAKE THE BISCUIT DUMPLINGS Meanwhile, in a medium bowl combine all the biscuit ingredients using a fork until the dough just comes together.

3 Dollop the biscuit dumplings on top of the sausage gravy. Secure the lid of the pressure cooker and set on Manual with low pressure for 4 minutes. Use natural release for 5 minutes, then quick release.

CRUSTLESS SOUTHWESTERN QUICHE

★ ★ ★

SERVES 4 TO 6
PREP TIME: 10 minutes
COOK TIME: 50 minutes

Think of this breakfast dish as a western omelet in quiche form. The pressure cooker works perfectly to cook the eggs with your favorite veggies or breakfast meats. The result is a quiche that everyone will love.

1½ cups water

Cooking spray, to grease

6 large eggs

⅓ cup low-fat milk

1 green bell pepper, stemmed, seeded, and small diced

1 garlic clove, minced

1 teaspoon fresh thyme or 2 teaspoons dried thyme

½ bunch scallions, thinly sliced, white and light green parts only

3 strips bacon, cooked, crumbled

¼ teaspoon cayenne pepper

¾ cup shredded pepper Jack

1 teaspoon kosher salt

½ teaspoon freshly ground black pepper

1 Place the steam rack in the bottom of the pressure cooker and add the water. Grease a 6-inch round cake pan or soufflé dish with cooking spray. Make a foil strap (see page 9) to go around the cake pan.

2 Whisk the eggs and milk together in a large bowl. Add the remaining ingredients and mix to combine. Pour into the cake pan, cover with a paper towel and then a piece of foil. Place in the pressure cooker, secure the lid, and cook on Manual with high pressure for 35 minutes. Allow to naturally release for 10 minutes, then quick release and remove the lid.

3 If you would like to brown the top of your quiche, preheat the broiler. Remove the quiche from the pressure cooker and place under the broiler until golden brown on top, 2 to 3 minutes. Remove and serve.

SWEET POTATO AND COLLARD HASH

★ ★ ★

SERVES 4
PREP TIME: 15 minutes
COOK TIME: 27 minutes

You can make a classic breakfast hash Southern style using sweet potatoes and collards! The pressure cooker cooks the potatoes and collard greens until just tender in half the time of traditional methods, so indulge on a Sunday—or even a Tuesday!

2 tablespoons olive oil

½ red onion, finely diced

1 garlic clove, minced

2 medium sweet potatoes, peeled, small diced

1 small bunch collards, stemmed and roughly chopped

½ teaspoon smoked sweet paprika

¼ teaspoon cayenne pepper

1 teaspoon kosher salt

½ teaspoon freshly ground black pepper

½ cup water

4 large eggs

½ cup grated Parmesan, to serve (optional)

1 Heat the olive oil in the pressure cooker on the Sauté setting. Add the onion and garlic and cook until almost translucent, about 4 minutes. Add the sweet potatoes and cook until golden, about 5 minutes. Add the collards, in batches if necessary, and cook until wilted, about 5 minutes. Add the paprika, cayenne, salt, and pepper and cook an additional minute. Add the water, secure the lid, and cook on Manual with high pressure for 6 minutes. Use quick release and remove the lid.

2 Return the pressure cooker to Sauté to recrisp the outside of the potatoes and reduce any excess liquid, about 3 minutes. Form four wells in the potato mixture and drop the eggs into the wells. Cook the eggs until the whites are solid but the yolk is still runny, 3 to 4 minutes. Serve with Parmesan, if desired.

VANILLA YOGURT
WITH HONEY AND PEACHES

★ ★ ★

Make this yogurt in large batches. You will find that it's perfect for breakfast, as a snack, or in a smoothie.

½ gallon whole or 2% milk

2 tablespoons plain yogurt with active cultures (to act as the yogurt starter)

2 teaspoons vanilla extract

½ vanilla bean, split and scraped

Peaches, pitted and thinly sliced, to serve

Honey, to serve

SERVES 8 TO 10
PREP TIME: 5 minutes
COOK TIME: 9 hours 30 minutes
+ cooling

TIP

Consult the pressure cooker manual for any questions on making yogurt.

NOTE

To sterilize jars, place heatproof jars in boiling water for 10 minutes. Remove from the water; allow to dry and cool completely before making yogurt.

1 Place the milk in the bowl of the electric pressure cooker. Select the Yogurt setting and press the Adjust button to place the pot on the "More" mode. This will boil the milk to a temperature of 180°F to pasteurize the milk. When the boiling process is done, the pot will beep and "Yogt" will be displayed on the screen.

2 Prepare an ice bath using a large heatproof bowl filled with ice and cold water. Carefully remove the metal insert of the pressure cooker and place in the ice bath while continuously stirring with a wooden spoon to cool the milk to a temperature below 115°F. Check the temperature using a thermometer throughout the stirring process. Remove from the ice bath and make sure to wipe the outside of the metal insert so that there is no water on the outside.

3 Once the milk has been cooled, place the plain yogurt in a large bowl and add 1 cup of the milk to the yogurt and whisk until combined to temper the yogurt starter. Add the yogurt starter mixture to the pot; add the vanilla extract and vanilla bean paste and mix to combine.

4 Place the metal insert into the pressure cooker, secure the lid, and place on Yogurt again. This will display a time of 8:00 hours. Cook the yogurt for 8 hours, then remove the lid. Place the yogurt in sterilized containers to cool in the refrigerator for several hours (see note).

5 Serve with sliced peaches and honey.

COCONUT YOGURT
WITH TOASTED ALMONDS

★ ★ ★

Making yogurt seems like a daunting task full of rules and regulations. But what if you could easily make homemade yogurt in your pressure cooker in just four easy steps? Give this coconut yogurt with toasted almonds a try. You won't be disappointed.

SERVES 8 TO 10
PREP TIME: 5 minutes
COOK TIME: 9 hours 30 minutes
+ cooling

TIP
Consult the pressure cooker manual for any questions on making yogurt.

½ gallon whole or 2% milk

2 tablespoons plain yogurt with active cultures (to act as the yogurt starter)

3 tablespoons coconut extract

¼ cup granola, to serve

Honey, to serve

Sliced almonds, toasted, to serve

Blueberries, to serve

1 Place the milk in the bowl of the electric pressure cooker. Select the Yogurt setting and press the Adjust button to place the pot on the "More" mode. This will boil the milk to a temperature of 180°F to pasteurize the milk. When the boiling process is done, the pot will beep and "Yogt" will be displayed on the screen.

2 Prepare an ice bath using a large heatproof bowl filled with ice and cold water. Carefully remove the metal insert of the pressure cooker and place in the ice bath while continuously stirring with a wooden spoon to cool the milk to a temperature below 115°F. Check the temperature using a thermometer throughout the stirring process. Remove from the ice bath and make sure to wipe the outside of the metal insert so that there is no water on the outside.

3 Once the milk has cooled, place the plain yogurt in a large bowl and add 1 cup of the milk to the yogurt and whisk until combined to temper the yogurt starter. Add the yogurt starter mixture back to the pot along with the coconut extract and mix to combine.

4 Place the metal insert into the pressure cooker, secure the lid, and select Yogurt again. This will display a time of 8:00 hours. Cook the yogurt for 8 hours, then remove the lid. Place the yogurt in sterilized containers to cool in the refrigerator for several hours (see note on page 39).

5 Serve the yogurt with honey, toasted almonds, and blueberries.

MAIN COURSES

★ ★ ★

PULLED PORK 44

SWEET AND SPICY BRAISED
BEEF BRISKET 48

SOUTHERN BARBECUE
RIBS 51

SWEET TEA PORK
TENDERLOIN 52

SUNDAY POT ROAST 56

CHICKEN AND
DUMPLINGS 59

BRUNSWICK STEW 62

JAMBALAYA 64

SHRIMP AND GRITS 66

SHRIMP BOIL 69

NEW ORLEANS BARBECUE
SHRIMP 71

CHICKEN AND SAUSAGE
GUMBO 72

BEEF AND SWEET POTATO
STEW 75

BEEF AND POBLANO
CHILI 79

SPICE-RUBBED ROAST
CHICKEN 81

KALE, ANDOUILLE, AND
WHITE BEAN STEW 82

SPICY TURKEY
SLOPPY JOES 84

CHICKEN NOODLE SOUP 87

COLA HONEY-GLAZED
HAM 89

CHILI LIME CHICKEN
DRUMSTICKS 90

PULLED PORK

★ ★ ★

Use this pulled pork to make a sandwich or as a topping on your favorite nachos or even in tacos! Forget watching the Dutch oven on the stove or in the oven, just place the meat in your pressure cooker, walk away, and come back to tender, juicy, and delicious pulled pork!

SERVES 6 TO 8

PREP TIME: 10 minutes + rub time
COOK TIME: 1 hour 25 minutes

SLOW COOKER
SETTING

Follow the method below. In step 2, add 2 cups of beef stock to the bottom of the pressure cooker after searing the pork. Once the lid is secure, select the Slow Cook high setting and cook for 6 to 7 hours or until the meat is tender enough to shred. Remove the meat from the pressure cooker and shred while the sauce is simmering.

FOR THE PULLED PORK

1 (4-pound) boneless pork shoulder, fat trimmed

2 tablespoons brown sugar

1½ tablespoons chili powder

1 tablespoon garlic powder

2 teaspoons onion powder

2 teaspoons cumin

2 teaspoons paprika

1 teaspoon cayenne pepper

2 teaspoons freshly ground black pepper

2 teaspoons kosher salt

2 tablespoons olive oil

1 cup beef stock

6–8 hamburger buns, warmed, to serve

FOR THE BARBECUE SAUCE

2 tablespoons olive oil

1 onion, small diced

2 cloves garlic, minced

½ cup water

1 tablespoon honey

1 teaspoon Worcestershire sauce

⅓ cup apple cider vinegar

½ cup ketchup

1 tablespoon Dijon mustard

1 **MAKE THE PULLED PORK** Cut the pork shoulder against the grain into three or four pieces to fit inside the pressure cooker. Combine all the spices in a small bowl. Rub all over the pork shoulder and allow to sit at room temperature for 30 minutes. (Preferably, rub, cover with plastic, and refrigerate for a few hours or up to overnight. Bring the pork to room temperature 30 minutes prior to cooking.)

continued

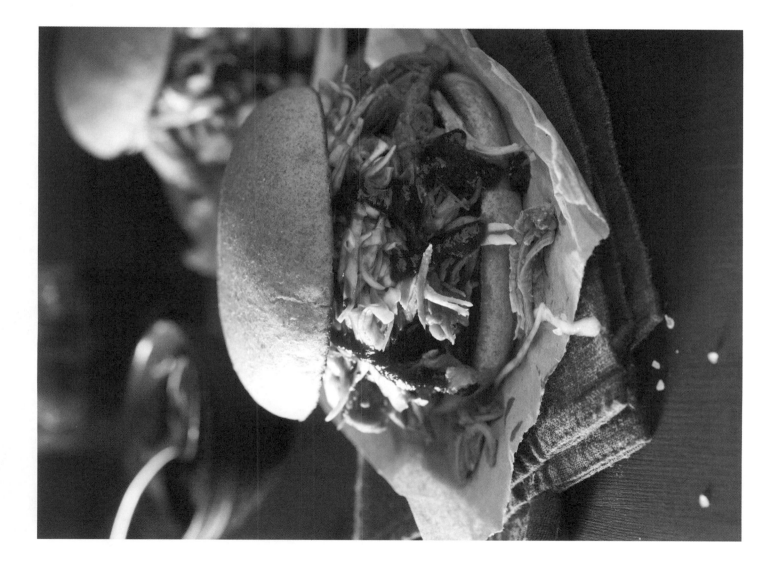

2 Select the Sauté setting and heat the olive oil. Sear the pieces of pork on all sides until browned. Add the beef stock, scraping up the browned bits from the bottom of the pan. Secure the lid and cook on Manual with high pressure for 55 minutes. Allow to naturally release for 10 minutes, then quick release. Remove the pork and shred with a fork. Discard the broth and wipe out the pot.

3 **MAKE THE BARBECUE SAUCE** Return the pressure cooker to the Sauté setting and add the olive oil. Add the onion and garlic and cook until almost translucent, about 4 minutes. Add the water, honey, Worcestershire sauce, vinegar, ketchup, and mustard and simmer until thickened, 5 to 7 minutes. Serve the sauce over the shredded meat or mix the meat and sauce together and serve on buns.

SWEET AND SPICY BRAISED BEEF BRISKET

★ ★ ★

SERVES 4 TO 6

PREP TIME: 15 minutes + rub time
COOK TIME: 1 hour 25 minutes

This brisket can be the showstopping main course for a Sunday dinner. Serve over mashed or roasted potatoes, with a vegetable mash, or even in a sandwich.

2 teaspoons kosher salt

1 tablespoon freshly ground black pepper

2 teaspoons garlic powder

1 teaspoon onion powder

1 tablespoon light brown sugar

1 tablespoon maple syrup

1 tablespoon honey

¼ teaspoon cayenne pepper

2 teaspoons Sriracha or hot sauce (page 131 or store bought)

1 (3- to 4-pound) brisket, trimmed

2 tablespoons olive oil

1 cup unsalted beef stock

1 tablespoon unsalted butter (optional)

¼ cup of water (if needed)

1 Combine the salt, black pepper, garlic powder, onion powder, brown sugar, maple syrup, honey, cayenne pepper, and Sriracha in a small bowl. Rub over the brisket. Allow the brisket to come to room temperature and set for at least 30 minutes. You can rub the brisket up to 12 hours in advance, wrapped tightly in plastic in the refrigerator. Be sure that the brisket comes to room temperature 30 minutes prior to cooking.

2 Select Sauté on the pressure cooker and heat the olive oil. Sear the brisket until browned on all sides. You may have to cut the brisket into two pieces and sear separately if it doesn't fit inside the pressure cooker. Transfer to a plate. Deglaze with beef stock, scraping the browned bits up from the bottom of the pot. Add the brisket back to the pot, secure the lid, and cook on Manual with high pressure for 55 minutes. Allow to naturally release for 10 minutes, then quick release and remove the lid.

3 Remove the brisket and allow to rest for 10 minutes tented with foil. Then slice against the grain. Discard half of the liquid in the pressure cook. Select Sauté on the pressure cooker and allow the remaining liquid to reduce until slightly thickened, about 7 minutes. Add the butter, if using, to the remaining sauce. If the sauce is too salty, add the water. Serve the sauce over the brisket.

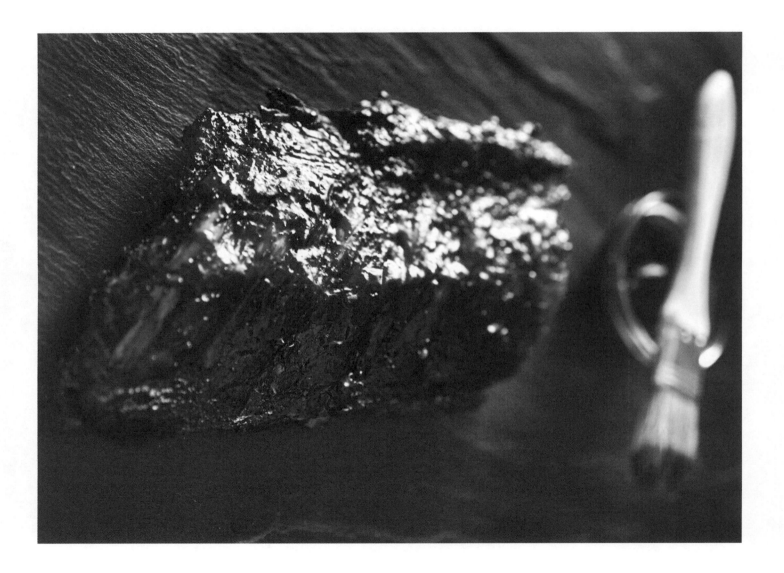

SOUTHERN BARBECUE RIBS

★ ★ ★

SERVES 4
PREP TIME: 10 minutes + rub time
COOK TIME: 40 minutes

Believe it or not, a pressure cooker can be used to make baby back ribs. Without the hassle of the grill, the pressure cooker keeps the ribs moist and cooks them until they are unbelievably tender. Just finish them under the broiler for a caramelization that everyone loves.

1 (4-pound) rack baby back ribs

1½ cups water

2 tablespoons chili powder

2 teaspoons kosher salt

2 teaspoons freshly ground black pepper

2 teaspoons garlic powder

2 teaspoons smoked paprika

1 teaspoon mustard powder

1 teaspoon celery salt

¼ teaspoon cayenne pepper

Barbecue sauce (page 136 or store bought)

1 Remove the membrane from the back of the baby back ribs. Cut into three or four pieces. Place the steam rack in the bottom of the electric pressure cooker and add the water.

2 Combine the remaining ingredients, except for the barbecue sauce, in a small bowl. Sprinkle evenly all over the ribs. Allow the ribs to sit with the spice mix for at least 15 minutes or wrapped in plastic overnight in the refrigerator. Place the ribs on the steam rack. Secure the lid and cook on Manual with high pressure for 25 minutes. Use natural release for 10 minutes, then quick release and remove the lid.

3 Preheat the oven to broil. Line a baking sheet with foil. Place the ribs on the baking sheet, brush both sides with barbecue sauce and place in the oven. Allow the sauce to slightly caramelize, about 2 minutes per side. Serve.

SWEET TEA PORK TENDERLOIN

★ ★ ★

SERVES 4

PREP TIME: 10 minutes
+ marinating time
COOK TIME: 30 minutes

This pork tenderloin gets all the flavors of the South from a delicious sweet tea sauce. It pairs well with roasted potatoes, vegetables, or even on top of a salad.

FOR THE MARINADE

1 pork tenderloin, trimmed

2 cups sweet tea

1 lemon, thinly sliced

1 teaspoon kosher salt

½ teaspoon freshly ground black pepper

1 teaspoon fresh thyme or 2 teaspoons dried thyme

FOR THE PORK TENDERLOIN

4 tablespoons olive oil, divided

Marinated pork tenderloin

1 shallot, minced

3 carrots, peeled and cut into ½-inch pieces on a bias

1 teaspoon kosher salt

1 teaspoon freshly ground black pepper, divided

1 cup sweet tea

2 tablespoons apple cider vinegar

½ cup Dijon mustard

2 teaspoons honey

1 teaspoon fresh thyme or 2 teaspoons dried thyme

1 **MARINATE THE PORK TENDERLOIN** In a large zip-top bag or baking dish, combine all of the marinade ingredients and marinate for at least 2 hours or overnight. When ready to cook, remove the tenderloin, discarding the marinade in the bag.

2 **MAKE THE PORK TENDERLOIN** Heat 2 tablespoons of the olive oil on the Sauté setting of the pressure cooker. Sear the pork tenderloin on all sides until browned, about 6 minutes, then transfer to a plate. You may have to cut the tenderloin into two pieces and sear separately if it doesn't fit inside the pressure cooker. Heat the remaining 2 tablespoons of olive oil on the Sauté setting of the pressure cooker. Add the shallot and carrots and cook until slightly tender, about 4 minutes. Season with the salt and ½ teaspoon of the pepper. Deglaze the bottom of the pot with sweet tea and add the apple cider vinegar. Combine the mustard, honey, thyme, and remaining ½ teaspoon pepper in a small bowl. Brush all over the tenderloin and place it in the sweet tea mixture.

3 Secure the lid and cook on Manual with high pressure for 12 minutes. Allow to naturally release for 5 minutes, then quick release and remove the lid. Check that the pork has reached an internal temperature of 145°F and is cooked through. If you need to cook the pork more, secure the lid of the pressure cooker again and set on high pressure for another 4 to 5 minutes. Then quick release and check the temperature.

4 Remove the tenderloin and carrots. Thinly slice the tenderloin and serve with carrots. Drizzle some of the sweet tea juices over the pork tenderloin to finish.

SUNDAY POT ROAST

★ ★ ★

Braise your classic Sunday pot roast with beer to take it up a Southern notch! And don't even think about cooking all day on Sunday anymore—let the pressure cooker do the work.

SERVES 4 TO 6

PREP TIME: 15 minutes
COOK TIME: 1 hour 10 minutes

SLOW COOKER SETTING

Follow the method below. For step 3, once the lid is secure, select Slow Cook high and cook for 6 to 7 hours or until tender. Add the potatoes, carrots, and mushrooms 1½ to 2 hours prior to the end of cooking. Transfer the meat and vegetables to a platter. Bring the sauce to a simmer and reduce to 1 cup, 6 to 7 minutes. Stir in the tablespoon of butter. Thinly slice the pot roast against the grain or shred depending on preference.

2 tablespoons olive oil, more if needed

1 (3-pound) boneless chuck roast, trimmed

2 teaspoons kosher salt, divided

1 teaspoon freshly ground black pepper, divided

1 large red onion, thinly sliced

2 garlic cloves, minced

1 teaspoon fresh thyme or 2 teaspoons dried thyme

¼ teaspoon ground cloves

1 (12-ounce) stout beer

½ pound baby Yukon Gold potatoes (about 6 potatoes), cut in half

4 carrots, peeled and cut in 1-inch pieces

8 ounces cremini mushrooms, quartered

1 tablespoon unsalted butter

Prepared quick-cooking grits, to serve (optional)

1 Heat the olive oil on the Sauté setting of the pressure cooker. Cut the chuck roast in half against the grain if too large to fit inside the pressure cooker. Season chuck roast with 1 teaspoon of the salt and ½ teaspoon of the pepper and sear on all sides until browned, about 7 minutes. Transfer to a plate.

2 Add more olive oil if necessary and add onion and garlic and cook until the onion is almost translucent, about 4 minutes. Add thyme, cloves, and season with remaining 1 teaspoon salt and ½ teaspoon pepper. Deglaze the pan with the stout beer, scraping up any browned bits from the bottom of the pan. Return the chuck roast to the pot.

continued

3 Secure the lid and cook on Manual with high pressure for 40 minutes. Allow to naturally release for 5 minutes, then quick release and remove the lid.

4 Remove the chuck roast to a carving board to rest and cover with foil. Add the potatoes, carrots, and mushrooms, secure the lid, and cook on high pressure for 5 minutes. Quick release, then remove the lid and transfer the vegetables to a platter.

5 Bring the sauce to a simmer using the Sauté setting and reduce to 1 cup, 6 to 7 minutes. Stir in the butter. Thinly slice or shred the pot roast. Serve with sauce, vegetables, and grits, if desired.

CHICKEN AND DUMPLINGS

★ ★ ★

This childhood classic, which usually takes hours to make, can be accomplished in under an hour with a pressure cooker. A store-bought baking mix keeps this recipe simple but delicious.

SERVES 4 TO 6

PREP TIME: 15 minutes
COOK TIME: 35 minutes

FOR THE CHICKEN

2 tablespoons olive oil

2 teaspoons kosher salt, divided

1 teaspoon freshly ground black pepper, divided

1 onion, thinly sliced

2 ribs celery, small diced

2 carrots, peeled and small diced

1 teaspoon fresh thyme or 2 teaspoons dried thyme

1 teaspoon fresh rosemary or 2 teaspoons dried rosemary

2 cups chicken stock

½ cup frozen peas, thawed

1 tablespoon unsalted butter, softened

1 tablespoon flour

⅓ cup heavy cream or milk

FOR THE DUMPLINGS

¾ cup baking mix, such as Bisquick

⅓ cup low-fat milk

1 teaspoon kosher salt

1 teaspoon freshly ground black pepper

½ teaspoon fresh thyme leaves or 1 teaspoon dried thyme leaves

1 **MAKE THE CHICKEN:** Select the Sauté setting on the pressure cooker and heat the olive oil. Season the chicken with 1 teaspoon of the salt and ½ teaspoon of the pepper and cook until browned on all sides, about 5 minutes. Transfer to a plate.

continued

2 Add the onion, celery, and carrots and cook until almost tender, about 4 minutes. Add the thyme, rosemary, remaining 1 teaspoon salt, and ½ teaspoon pepper and cook for another minute. Add the chicken and chicken stock, secure the lid, and cook on Manual with low pressure for 8 minutes.

3 **MAKE THE DUMPLINGS:** Meanwhile, combine all the dumpling ingredients in a medium bowl using the prongs of a fork until just combined.

4 Use quick release on the pressure cooker and return to the Sauté setting. Stir in the peas.

5 Mix the butter and flour together with your hands in a small bowl. Whisk into the broth and allow to thicken, about 5 minutes.

6 Drop the dumpling mixture by the spoonful into the pot. Simmer the dumplings for 8 to 10 minutes until cooked through. Stir in the heavy cream and serve.

BRUNSWICK STEW

★ ★ ★

Coming home on a cold day and craving hot soup? No worries, this Southern classic will be on the table in less than 45 minutes!

SERVES 4

PREP TIME: 15 minutes
COOK TIME: 40 minutes

SLOW COOKER
SETTING

Follow the steps below and add an additional cup of chicken broth to the stew in step 2. For step 3, secure the lid and select the Slow Cook low setting and cook for 5 to 6 hours. Add the corn, lima beans, and okra, if using, 1 hour before serving.

2 tablespoons olive oil

1 pound boneless pork shoulder, trimmed and cut into 1-inch pieces

1 pound boneless, skinless chicken breast, cut into 1-inch pieces

2 teaspoons kosher salt, divided

1 teaspoon freshly ground black pepper, divided

2 stalks celery, thinly sliced

½ red onion, small diced

2 garlic cloves, minced

1 green bell pepper, stemmed, seeded, and small diced

¼ teaspoon cayenne pepper

1 tablespoon flour

1 cup chicken broth

1 (15-ounce) can crushed tomatoes

½ cup barbecue sauce (page 136 or store bought)

1 cup frozen corn, thawed

1 cup frozen lima beans, thawed

1 cup frozen sliced okra, thawed (optional)

1 Heat the olive oil in the pressure cooker on the Sauté setting. Season the pork and chicken with 1 teaspoon of the salt and ½ teaspoon of the pepper. Sear the pork and chicken, in batches if necessary, until browned on all sides and remove to a plate.

2 Add the celery, onion, garlic, and bell pepper and cook until almost tender, about 4 minutes. Season with remaining 1 teaspoon salt and ½ teaspoon pepper, add the cayenne and flour, and stir to coat the vegetables. Add the chicken broth and deglaze the pot, scraping the browned bits up from the bottom. Add the crushed tomatoes and barbecue sauce and bring to a simmer. Return the pork and chicken to the pot.

3 Secure the lid and set on Manual with high pressure for 12 minutes. Allow to naturally release for 10 minutes, then quick release and remove the lid. Return to the Sauté setting and add the corn, lima beans, and okra, if using, and stir to combine. Simmer for another 2 minutes.

JAMBALAYA

★ ★ ★

Bring the flair of New Orleans into your kitchen with this easy jambalaya. The combination of andouille sausage and shrimp with tender rice that cooks in close to 20 minutes will make you want to prepare this recipe from The Big Easy all the time.

2 tablespoons olive oil

8 ounces andouille sausage, thinly sliced

1 onion, finely diced

3 celery stalks, finely diced

1 green bell pepper, stemmed, seeded, and finely diced

2 garlic cloves, minced

1 teaspoon fresh thyme or 2 teaspoons dried thyme

1 teaspoon fresh oregano or 2 teaspoons dried oregano

1 teaspoon paprika

¼ teaspoon cayenne pepper

½ teaspoon onion powder

1 teaspoon kosher salt

½ teaspoon freshly ground black pepper

1¼ cups long grain white rice

1 (14-ounce) can crushed tomatoes

2½ cups chicken stock, divided

¾ pound medium shrimp, peeled and deveined, tails on

Scallions, thinly sliced, to garnish

SERVES 4

PREP TIME: 15 minutes
COOK TIME: 35 minutes

SLOW COOKER
SETTING

Cook the rice in advance according to package instructions. Follow the steps below, but do not add the rice in step 1. Secure the lid and select the Slow Cook low setting and cook for 5 to 6 hours. Store the cooked sausage in the refrigerator in the meantime. Add the rice, shrimp, and sausage 10 minutes prior to serving.

1 Heat the olive oil using the Sauté setting of the pressure cooker. Add the sausage and cook until browned, about 6 minutes. Transfer to a paper towel–lined plate. Add the onion, celery, green bell pepper, and garlic and cook until the vegetables have slightly softened, about 5 minutes. Add the thyme, oregano, paprika, cayenne, onion powder, salt, and pepper and stir to combine. Add the rice, crushed tomatoes, and 1½ cups of the chicken stock.

2 Secure the lid and set on Manual with high pressure for 8 minutes. Allow to naturally release for 10 minutes, then quick release.

3 Return the pressure cooker to the Sauté setting and add the remaining 1 cup of stock and the shrimp. Simmer until the shrimp are pink and opaque, about 3 minutes. Add the sausage back to the pot, stir to combine, and garnish with scallions.

SHRIMP AND GRITS

★ ★ ★

The classic Southern breakfast, lunch, or dinner favorite can be made in your pressure cooker! Use your preferred vegetables and sausage, and add cheese to the grits for an even creamier dish.

SERVES 4
PREP TIME: 15 minutes
COOK TIME: 25 minutes

2 tablespoons olive oil

3 slices bacon, roughly chopped

1 onion, finely chopped

1 green bell pepper, seeded, and finely diced

2 garlic cloves, minced

1 teaspoon kosher salt

½ teaspoon freshly ground black pepper

1 lemon, juiced

1 teaspoon Worcestershire sauce

1 cup yellow stone-ground grits

2⅔ cups chicken stock, divided

1 (14-ounce) can crushed tomatoes

¾ pound medium shrimp, peeled and deveined, tails on

Scallions, thinly sliced, to garnish

Hot sauce (page 131 or store bought), to serve

1 Heat the olive oil using the Sauté setting of the pressure cooker. Add the bacon and cook until browned and crisp, about 6 minutes. Transfer the bacon to a paper towel–lined plate and remove half the bacon fat from the pot and discard. Add the onion, green bell pepper, and garlic and cook until almost tender, about 4 minutes. Season with salt and pepper. Add the lemon juice, Worcestershire sauce, grits, 2 cups of the chicken stock, and crushed tomatoes.

2 Secure the lid and cook on Manual with low pressure for 10 minutes. Naturally release for 10 minutes, then quick release.

3 Return the pressure cooker to Sauté, and add the remaining ⅔ cup of stock and the shrimp. Cook until the shrimp are pink and opaque, about 3 minutes. Add the bacon back to the pot, garnish with scallions, and serve with hot sauce.

SHRIMP BOIL

★ ★ ★

Throw a dinner party with this classic Southern communal recipe. Gather your favorite seafood, in this case shrimp, and spices for a boil that everyone will love. With a pressure cooker, this boil can be prepared in almost no time.

SERVES 4 TO 6
PREP TIME: 15 minutes
COOK TIME: 15 minutes

2 tablespoons olive oil

8 ounces andouille sausage, sliced ¼-inch thick

4 cups water

3 tablespoons Old Bay Seasoning

2 bay leaves

2 lemons, halved and juiced

2 cloves garlic, smashed

1 teaspoon black peppercorns

2 tablespoons kosher salt

1 pound baby new potatoes, halved

2 ears corn, shucked and cut into three pieces

2 pounds medium shrimp, unpeeled

Hot sauce (page 131 or store bought), to serve

1 Select the Sauté setting on the pressure cooker and heat the olive oil. Add the sausage and cook until browned on all sides, about 7 minutes. Transfer to a plate.

2 Add water, Old Bay Seasoning, bay leaves, lemon juice and squeezed lemon halves, garlic, black peppercorns, salt, potatoes, and corn. Secure the lid and cook on Manual with high pressure for 5 minutes. Use quick release and remove the lid.

3 Return the pressure cooker to Sauté setting and add the shrimp. Simmer until the shrimp are pink and opaque, about 3 minutes. Serve with hot sauce.

NEW ORLEANS BARBECUE SHRIMP

★ ★ ★

The pressure cooker steams the shrimp to perfection. Serve over Carolina long-grain rice or grits to capture all of the buttery, robust flavors.

SERVES 4 TO 6

PREP TIME: 5 minutes
COOK TIME: 5 minutes

¾ cup barbecue sauce (page 136 or store bought)

2 tablespoons unsalted butter

2 teaspoons hot sauce (page 131 or store bought)

⅓ cup water or chicken stock

2½ pounds large shrimp, unpeeled, heads on or removed

Prepared Carolina rice or grits, to serve

Lemon wedges, to serve

1 Select the Sauté setting on the pressure cooker. Add the barbecue sauce, butter, hot sauce, and chicken stock and warm through just until the butter melts. Add the shrimp, secure the lid, and cook on Manual with high pressure for 2 minutes. Use quick release and remove the lid.

2 Serve the shrimp over Carolina rice or grits with lemon wedges.

CHICKEN AND SAUSAGE GUMBO

★ ★ ★

Fill your kitchen with the smells of a classic Southern stew. For a variation, use a combination of chicken, sausage, and any type of seafood in this recipe.

SERVES 4

PREP TIME: 15 minutes
COOK TIME: 30 minutes

7 tablespoons olive oil, divided

8 ounces andouille sausage, cut into ¼-inch slices

4 boneless, skinless chicken thighs, cut into 1-inch pieces

2 teaspoons kosher salt, divided

1½ teaspoons freshly ground black pepper, divided

⅓ cup flour

1 green bell pepper, stemmed, seeded, and finely diced

1 onion, finely diced

2 ribs celery, finely diced

2 cloves garlic, minced

1 teaspoon fresh thyme or 2 teaspoons dried thyme

1 teaspoon paprika

¼ teaspoon cayenne pepper

¼ teaspoon allspice

2 teaspoons Worcestershire sauce

1 (15-ounce) can diced tomatoes

1½ cups chicken stock

White rice, cooked, to serve

Scallions, thinly sliced, to serve

Hot sauce (page 131 or store bought), to serve

1. Select the Sauté setting on the pressure cooker and heat 2 tablespoons of the olive oil. Add the sausage and cook until browned on both sides, about 5 minutes. Transfer to a plate.

2. Season the chicken with 1 teaspoon of the salt and ½ teaspoon of the pepper. Cook until browned on all sides, about 7 minutes, then transfer to a plate.

3. Add the remaining 5 tablespoons of olive oil and the flour. Cook, stirring constantly, until the flour turns the color of

continued

peanut butter, about 5 minutes. Be careful not to burn yourself—the oil is hot! Add the bell pepper, onion, celery, and garlic and cook until slightly softened, about 3 minutes. Add the thyme, paprika, cayenne, allspice, Worcestershire, remaining 1 teaspoon salt, and 1 teaspoon pepper and cook another minute. Add the diced tomatoes, chicken stock, chicken, and sausage.

4 Secure the lid and cook on Manual with high pressure for 8 minutes. Use quick release, serve over white rice, and garnish with scallions, with hot sauce on the side.

BEEF AND SWEET POTATO STEW

★ ★ ★

The cooking time for this beef stew is only a half hour! Tender and delicious, this meal is made with just one pot.

SERVES 4
PREP TIME: 20 minutes
COOK TIME: 40 minutes

SLOW COOKER SETTING

Follow the instructions below through step 3, then secure the lid and place on the Slow Cook low setting for 7 to 9 hours until the beef and potatoes are tender. Then use step 5 as necessary.

2 tablespoons olive oil

1½ pounds stew meat such as chuck roast, cut into 1-inch cubes

1 teaspoon kosher salt

½ teaspoon freshly ground black pepper

3 tablespoons flour

1 teaspoon paprika

1 red onion, diced

1 (8-ounce) box cremini mushrooms, sliced

2 garlic cloves, minced

2 carrots, peeled and cut into ½-inch pieces

2 ribs celery, chopped

2 teaspoons dried rosemary leaves

1 teaspoon dried thyme leaves

¼ teaspoon ground cloves

⅓ cup red wine

2 medium sweet potatoes, peeled and cut into 1-inch pieces

2 teaspoons Worcestershire sauce

1 cup beef stock

1 tablespoon flour (if needed)

1 tablespoon unsalted butter, softened (if needed)

1 Select the Sauté setting and heat the olive oil.

2 Season the beef with salt and pepper. Place flour and paprika in a baking dish and dredge beef in flour, shaking off any excess. Add the beef to the pot and brown on all sides, about 6 minutes, working in batches, if necessary. Transfer the beef to a plate.

3 Add the onion, mushrooms, and garlic and cook until tender and golden brown, about 5 minutes. Add the carrots, celery, rosemary, thyme, and cloves and cook another 2 minutes. Deglaze

continued

the pan with red wine, scraping the browned bits off the bottom of the pot. Add the sweet potatoes, Worcestershire sauce, and beef stock. Stir and secure with the lid.

4 Cook on Manual with high pressure for 12 minutes. Use natural release and serve.

5 If the stew is too thin, combine the flour and butter in a small bowl and mix together to form a paste. Select Sauté on the electric pressure cooker and add the flour mixture. Whisk to combine and simmer until thickened, about 4 minutes. Serve.

BEEF AND POBLANO CHILI

★ ★ ★

It's a cold winter night and all you can think about is chili . . . but you realize it's going to take a few hours to make. With the pressure cooker you can make your favorite chili just minutes before you eat it. Choose your favorite meats, veggies, and spices to customize this comforting winter dish.

SERVES 4
PREP TIME: 15 minutes
COOK TIME: 35 minutes

———◆———

SLOW COOKER
SETTING

Follow the steps below. In step 2, when ready to secure the lid, select the Slow Cook low setting and allow to cook for 7 to 8 hours. Add the beans during the last 30 minutes of cooking.

2 tablespoons olive oil

1 pound ground sirloin

1 teaspoon kosher salt

½ teaspoon freshly ground black pepper

2 poblanos, stemmed, seeded, and small diced

1 red onion, small diced

1 jalapeño, thinly sliced

2 garlic cloves, minced

2 tablespoons chili powder

2 teaspoons cumin

¼ teaspoon cayenne pepper

1 (12-ounce) lager beer

½ cup beef stock or water

1 (15-ounce) can diced tomatoes

2 (15-ounce) cans red kidney beans, drained and rinsed

Scallions, thinly sliced, to garnish

Shredded Cheddar, to garnish

Sour cream, to garnish

1 Select Sauté on the pressure cooker and add the olive oil. Add the ground sirloin and cook until browned, about 7 minutes. Season with salt and pepper. Add the poblanos, onion, jalapeño, and garlic and cook until almost tender, about 5 minutes. Add the chili powder, cumin, and cayenne and cook another minute. Deglaze with the beer, scraping up the browned bits from the bottom of the pan. Add the beef stock and diced tomatoes.

2 Secure the lid and cook on Manual with high pressure for 15 minutes. Use quick release and return the pressure cooker to the Sauté setting. Add the beans and simmer until warmed through, about 5 minutes. Garnish with scallions, cheese, and sour cream.

SPICE-RUBBED ROAST CHICKEN

★ ★ ★

SERVES 4 TO 6

PREP TIME: 10 minutes
COOK TIME: 35 minutes

Looking for that crazy tender and juicy roast chicken recipe? The pressure cooker makes a chicken that is perfectly moist and not overcooked. Crisp the skin in the oven before serving for the ultimate roast chicken.

1 tablespoon smoked paprika

1 tablespoon cumin

1 tablespoon garlic powder

2 teaspoons freshly ground black pepper, divided

2 teaspoons kosher salt, divided

1 tablespoon light brown sugar

½ teaspoon cayenne pepper

2 tablespoons olive oil

1 (3- to 4-pound) chicken, wishbone removed

½ cup chicken stock

½ cup lager-style beer

Hot sauce (page 131 or store bought), to serve

1 Combine the smoked paprika, cumin, garlic powder, 1 teaspoon black pepper, 1 teaspoon salt, brown sugar, and cayenne in a small bowl and set aside.

2 Heat a large sauté pan over medium-high heat and add the olive oil. Season the chicken with remaining salt and pepper and tie the legs together with kitchen twine. Sear the chicken on all sides until golden brown, about 10 minutes. Remove and set aside.

3 Place the steam rack inside of the pressure cooker. Add the chicken stock and beer. Rub the chicken with the spice rub and place in the pressure cooker on top of the steam rack. Secure the lid and set on Manual with high pressure for 18 minutes. Allow to naturally release for 5 minutes, then quick release and remove the lid.

4 Preheat the broiler. Transfer the chicken to a baking sheet lined with foil. Crisp the skin under the broiler, 3 to 4 minutes. Serve with hot sauce.

KALE, ANDOUILLE, AND WHITE BEAN STEW

★ ★ ★

This dish is perfect for a cold day or when you're feeling under the weather. The spice of the cayenne combined with the greens and beans makes for a stew that will leave you feeling warm and satisfied.

SERVES 4 TO 6

PREP TIME: 15 minutes
COOK TIME: 40 minutes

SLOW COOKER
SETTING

Follow the steps below. For step 2, once the lid is secure, select the Slow Cook low setting and cook for 6 hours.

2 tablespoons olive oil

8 ounces andouille sausage, sliced ¼-inch thick

1 yellow onion, small diced

2 carrots, peeled and thinly sliced

2 cloves garlic, minced

1 teaspoon crushed red pepper flakes

1 teaspoon kosher salt

½ teaspoon freshly ground black pepper

1 teaspoon fresh thyme or 2 teaspoons dried thyme

1 bunch lacinato (dinosaur) kale, stems removed and roughly chopped

1 pound baby Yukon Gold potatoes, halved

1 (15-ounce) can diced tomatoes

3 cups chicken stock

1 (15-ounce) can cannellini beans, drained and rinsed

1 Heat the pressure cooker on the Sauté setting and add the olive oil. Add the sausage and cook until browned, about 6 minutes. Add the onion and carrots and cook until almost translucent, about 4 minutes. Add the garlic, red pepper flakes, salt, pepper, and thyme and cook for an additional minute. Add the kale and allow to wilt slightly. Add the potatoes, tomatoes, and chicken stock.

2 Secure the lid and cook on Manual with high pressure for 20 minutes. Allow to naturally release for 5 minutes, then quick release and remove the lid.

3 Return the pressure cooker to the Sauté setting and add the cannellini beans. Allow to simmer until warmed through, about 2 minutes, and serve.

SPICY TURKEY SLOPPY JOES

★ ★ ★

This childhood classic with a homemade sauce is made quickly and mess free in your pressure cooker. Using ground turkey instead of beef lightens up these sloppy joes.

2 tablespoons olive oil

1½ pounds ground turkey

1 red onion, finely chopped

1 green bell pepper, stemmed, seeded, and finely chopped

2 cloves garlic, minced

2 teaspoons smoked sweet paprika

½ teaspoon cayenne pepper

1 teaspoon kosher salt

½ teaspoon freshly ground black pepper

1 tablespoon tomato paste

1 (15-ounce) can crushed tomatoes

⅓ cup dark brown sugar

2 teaspoons Worcestershire sauce

1 tablespoon Dijon mustard

4 sesame seed or wheat buns

4 slices Cheddar or American cheese (optional)

SERVES 4

PREP TIME: 15 minutes
COOK TIME: 25 minutes

SLOW COOKER
SETTING

Follow the steps below. For step 2, once the lid is secure, select the Slow Cook low setting and cook for 5 to 6 hours. Continue with step 3 once finished slow cooking.

1. Select the Sauté setting and heat the olive oil. Add the ground turkey and cook until browned, about 7 minutes. Add the onion and bell pepper and cook until almost tender, about 4 minutes. Add the garlic, paprika, cayenne, salt, and pepper and cook for an additional minute. Add the tomato paste and cook for 1 minute until slightly caramelized. Add the tomatoes, brown sugar, and Worcestershire sauce.

2. Secure the lid and cook on Manual with low pressure for 8 minutes. Allow to naturally release for 5 minutes, then quick release and remove lid.

3. Stir in the Dijon mustard. If the sauce is too runny, select the Sauté setting and reduce until thickened.

4. Serve on buns with a slice of cheese, if desired.

CHICKEN NOODLE SOUP

★ ★ ★

This cure-all of soups made with your favorite vegetables can be ready in about 30 minutes. Forget purchasing it from the supermarket or a local cafe, make this homemade soup in batches and freeze for an easy weeknight meal.

2 tablespoons olive oil

1 onion, finely diced

2 cloves garlic, minced

2 stalks celery, thinly sliced

2 carrots, peeled and thinly sliced

1 teaspoon fresh thyme or 2 teaspoons dried thyme

1 teaspoon kosher salt

½ teaspoon freshly ground black pepper

2 boneless, skinless chicken breasts

2 boneless, skinless chicken thighs

3 cups chicken stock, divided

½ (12-ounce) bag of egg noodles

Parsley, chopped, to garnish

SERVES 4 TO 6

PREP TIME: 15 minutes
COOK TIME: 18 minutes

———◆———

SLOW COOKER
SETTING

Follow the steps below. For step 2, once the lid is secure, select the Slow Cook low setting and cook for 6 hours. Shred the chicken during the last 15 minutes of cooking and add the egg noodles. Garnish with parsley.

1 Select the Sauté setting and heat the olive oil. Add the onion, garlic, celery, and carrots and cook until almost tender, about 4 minutes. Add the thyme, salt, and pepper and stir to combine. Add the chicken breasts and thighs and 1½ cups of the chicken stock.

2 Secure the lid and cook on Manual with high pressure for 8 minutes. Use quick release, remove the lid, and shred the chicken.

3 Return the pressure cooker to Sauté setting and add the remaining 1½ cups chicken stock and egg noodles to the soup. Simmer for 5 minutes until the egg noodles are cooked through. Serve and garnish with parsley.

COLA HONEY-GLAZED HAM

★ ★ ★

Why not try making a sweet glazed ham in your pressure cooker? You can prepare this ham in a quarter of the time that it normally takes, and without the mess! This is a great recipe to try when holiday season comes around and you are dreading the preparation of this traditionally time-consuming dish.

SERVES 4 TO 6

PREP TIME: 15 minutes
COOK TIME: 25 minutes

1 (6- to 7-pound) boneless ham, fully cooked

¼ cup honey

¼ cup molasses

1 orange, zested and juiced

1 cup cola

2 teaspoons kosher salt

1 teaspoon freshly ground black pepper

¼ cup whole cloves

1½ cups water

1 Score the ham in a crisscross direction to form a diamond pattern.

2 Select the Sauté setting on the pressure cooker. Add the honey, molasses, orange zest, orange juice, and cola and mix to combine. Season with salt and pepper. Allow to reduce for 8 to 10 minutes until the liquid thickens and coats the back of a spoon. Transfer to a bowl and clean out the pot.

3 Brush three-quarters of the honey mixture all over the ham. Insert the whole cloves at the top and bottom of the diamonds.

4 Place the steam rack inside of the pressure cooker and add the water. Wrap the ham in foil and place on top of the steam rack. Secure the lid and cook on Manual with high pressure for 10 minutes. Allow to naturally release for 5 minutes, then quick release and remove the lid.

5 Remove the ham and brush with the remaining honey glaze one last time before serving.

CHILI LIME CHICKEN DRUMSTICKS

★ ★ ★

Perfect for a tailgate party or summer outdoor barbecue, the delicious flavors of chili and lime give these drumsticks a spicy Tex-Mex flair.

SERVES 4 TO 6

PREP TIME: 10 minutes
COOK TIME: 25 minutes

2 tablespoons olive oil

2 pounds chicken drumsticks

1 teaspoon kosher salt

½ teaspoon freshly ground black pepper

½ cup chicken stock

2 teaspoons ancho or regular chili powder

1 lime, zested and juiced

1 teaspoon honey

1 Fresno chili pepper, thinly sliced (seeded if desired)

Cilantro leaves, to garnish

1 Select the Sauté setting and heat the olive oil. Season the chicken with salt and pepper and sear until browned on all sides; you may need to do this in batches if necessary. Transfer the drumsticks to a plate. Deglaze the pan with the chicken stock.

2 In a small bowl combine the chili powder, lime zest and juice, honey, and Fresno chili and mix to combine. Divide in half into two small bowls. Brush half of the chili powder mixture all over the chicken. Return the chicken to the pressure cooker.

3 Secure the lid and cook on Manual with high pressure for 15 minutes, and use quick release. The chicken should register 165°F on a meat thermometer. If additional cooking is needed, secure the lid and place on Manual with high pressure for another 4 minutes. Use quick release and check the temperature again.

4 Preheat the broiler and line a baking sheet with foil.

5 Transfer the chicken from the pressure cooker to the prepared baking sheet and brush with the remaining half of the chili powder mixture. Place under the broiler and cook until warmed through and skin is crispy, about 3 minutes. Garnish with cilantro.

SNACKS AND SIDES

★ ★ ★

CAJUN BOILED PEANUTS

★ ★ ★

This classic Southern snack can be made in less than an hour with your pressure cooker. Use your favorite seasonings to spice up your peanut mix!

SERVES 4 TO 6
PREP TIME: 5 minutes
COOK TIME: 50 minutes

1½ pounds peanuts in the shell

¼ cup kosher salt

⅓ cup Cajun seasoning, such as McCormick

1 Sort the peanuts, discarding any debris, and rinse.

2 Place the peanuts in the pressure cooker. Add salt, Cajun seasoning, and water to cover. Place the steam rack on top of the peanuts to help keep them submerged in the water. Secure the lid and place on Manual with high pressure for 45 minutes. Allow to naturally release for 5 minutes, then quick release and remove the lid. Serve warm or at room temperature.

HOT CHICKEN WINGS

★ ★ ★

SERVES 4

PREP TIME: 5 minutes
COOK TIME: 25 minutes

Everyone's favorite tailgating snack just got easier! Make these hot chicken wings in the electric pressure cooker in no time and finish them in the oven for a tender, crispy, and spicy snack everyone will love!

2 pounds chicken wings, tips removed

2 tablespoons olive oil

1 teaspoon kosher salt

½ teaspoon freshly ground black pepper

1½ cups water

½ stick unsalted butter, melted

1 cup hot sauce (page 131 or store bought)

Scallions, thinly sliced, to garnish

1 Select the Sauté function and heat the olive oil. Season the chicken wings with salt and pepper. Sear the wings on all sides until browned and remove to a plate. Deglaze the pan with the water and place the steam rack inside of the pressure cooker. Place the wings on top of the steam rack.

2 Secure the lid and place on Manual with high pressure for 8 minutes. Use quick release and remove the lid. Check to make sure that the wings are cooked through or a meat thermometer reads 165°F. If not, secure the lid again, place on high pressure for another 4 minutes, and check again.

3 Meanwhile, preheat the oven to 450°F and line a baking sheet with foil.

4 Combine the butter and hot sauce in a large bowl. Remove the wings from the pressure cooker and toss in the hot sauce. Transfer to the baking sheet and place in the oven for 5 to 7 minutes until the sauce warms through and the skin of the wings becomes crispy. Remove from the oven, garnish with scallions, and serve.

COLLARDS AND ARTICHOKE DIP

★ ★ ★

Spinach and artichoke dip, that classic cheesy appetizer, is turned Southern with collards. Making this crazy-delicious snack is the perfect way to use up leftover greens. Mix the filling together and freeze in advance. Just thaw and cook in the pressure cooker before serving!

SERVES 4 TO 6

PREP TIME: 20 minutes
COOK TIME: 20 minutes

SLOW COOKER
SETTING

Follow the method below. For step 4, once the lid is secure, select the Slow Cook low setting and allow to cook for 2 hours or until the dip is warm and the cheese is melted. Proceed with step 5 to finish.

2 tablespoons olive oil

1 bunch collards, stems removed and leaves roughly chopped

2 cloves garlic, minced

2 teaspoons kosher salt, divided

1 teaspoon freshly ground black pepper, divided

1½ cups water

Cooking spray, for greasing pan

1 (8-ounce) package cream cheese, softened

⅓ cup mayonnaise

¼ cup sour cream

1 can artichoke hearts, drained and quartered

¼ teaspoon cayenne pepper

1 cup shredded Parmesan

Paprika, optional, to garnish

Crusty bread and crudité, to serve

1 Heat a large sauté pan with the olive oil over medium-high heat. Add the collards and cook until wilted and almost tender, 8 to 10 minutes. Add the garlic and season with 1 teaspoon of the salt and ½ teaspoon of the pepper. Remove from the heat and allow to cool.

2 Place the steam rack in the pressure cooker and add the water. Grease a 7-inch round baking dish with cooking spray.

3 Combine the cream cheese, mayonnaise, sour cream, artichoke hearts, cayenne, remaining salt and pepper, and collard mixture and mix to combine. Transfer to the baking dish and cover with foil. Place in the pressure cooker.

4 Secure the lid and place on Manual with high pressure for 8 minutes. Allow to naturally release for 5 minutes, then quick release and remove the lid.

5 Preheat the oven to broil. Remove the foil and sprinkle with cheese. Place under the broiler until the cheese is melted and golden brown, 3 to 4 minutes. Sprinkle the top with paprika, if desired, and serve with crusty bread and crudité.

PIMENTO CHEESE DIP

★ ★ ★

The classic Southern cheese spread, made with mayonnaise, shredded cheddar, and pimentos, is now a creamy, warm dip. This easy-to-make dish is great to serve at tailgate parties!

1½ cups water

8 ounces sharp Cheddar, shredded

8 ounces Monterey Jack, shredded

4 ounces cream cheese, softened and cut into cubes

½ cup mayonnaise

1 (4-ounce) jar pimentos, drained and chopped

¼ teaspoon cayenne pepper

½ teaspoon kosher salt

¼ teaspoon freshly ground black pepper

Parsley, finely chopped, to garnish

Buttery crackers, to serve

Crostini, to serve

Crudité, such as carrot sticks, celery sticks, and radishes, to serve

SERVES 4 TO 6

PREP TIME: 15 minutes
COOK TIME: 8 minutes

SLOW COOKER SETTING

Follow the method below. For step 3, once the lid is secure, select the Slow Cook low setting and allow to cook for 2 hours or until the dip is warm and cheese is melted. Proceed with step 4 to finish.

1 Place the steam rack in the bottom of the pressure cooker and add the water.

2 Combine the cheeses, mayonnaise, pimentos, cayenne pepper, salt, and black pepper in a large bowl and mix together until the ingredients just come together. Transfer to a 6-inch round baking dish and place the dish on top of the steam rack. Cover the baking dish with foil.

3 Secure the lid and place on Manual with high pressure for 8 minutes. Allow to naturally release for 5 minutes, then quick release and remove the lid. The cheese should be melted. If the cheese is not completely melted, secure the lid again on the pressure cooker and place on Manual with high pressure for another 3 minutes. Remove the lid and check again.

 If desired, preheat the broiler. Place the cheese dip underneath the broiler until golden brown and bubbling on top, 4 to 5 minutes.

5 Garnish with parsley and serve with buttery crackers, crostini, and crudité.

SEVEN LAYER DIP

★ ★ ★

This is the perfect appetizer for any party. Simply layer your favorite Mexican ingredients to make a warm version of seven layer dip that takes snacking to another level!

SERVES 4 TO 6
PREP TIME: 15 minutes
COOK TIME: 15 minutes

SLOW COOKER
SETTING

Follow the method below. For step 4, once the lid is secure, select the Slow Cook low setting and cook for 2 hours or until the dip is warm and cheese is melted. Proceed with step 5 to finish.

2 tablespoons olive oil

1 red onion, small diced

1 jalapeño, seeded and minced

2 cloves garlic, minced

1 teaspoon cumin

1 teaspoon kosher salt

½ teaspoon freshly ground black pepper

1½ cups water

Cooking spray, to grease

1 (15-ounce) can refried beans

2 limes, zested and juiced

1 (8-ounce) block cream cheese

1½ cups fresh or frozen corn, thawed

1 cup shredded Monterey Jack

½ cup shredded sharp Cheddar

Cilantro, optional, to garnish

Tortilla chips, to serve

1 Heat a large sauté pan with the olive oil over medium heat. Add the onion, jalapeño, and garlic and cook until almost translucent, about 4 minutes. Add the cumin, salt, and pepper and cook an additional minute. Allow to cool slightly.

2 Place the steam rack inside of the pressure cooker and fill with water. Grease a 7-inch round baking or soufflé dish with cooking spray.

3 Mix the refried beans with the lime zest and juice in a medium bowl and spread into the bottom of the baking dish. In a separate medium bowl mix the cream cheese with the onion mixture and corn and spread on top of the refried beans. Top with Monterey Jack and Cheddar. Wrap with foil and place in the pressure cooker.

4 Secure the lid and place on Manual with high pressure for 10 minutes. Allow to naturally release for 5 minutes, then quick release.

5 Remove, garnish with cilantro, and serve with tortilla chips.

SPICY CRAB DIP

★ ★ ★

Bring the ocean to you with this spicy crab dip. Your favorite flavors from the coast can be made into a warm, creamy dip in just minutes.

SERVES 4
PREP TIME: 10 minutes
COOK TIME: 15 minutes

1½ cups water

Cooking spray, for greasing pan

1 (8-ounce) package cream cheese, softened

⅓ cup mayonnaise

1 lemon, zested and juiced

½ bunch scallions, thinly sliced

2 teaspoons Dijon mustard

1 teaspoon kosher salt

½ teaspoon freshly ground black pepper

2 teaspoons Old Bay seasoning

¼ teaspoon cayenne pepper

1 (8-ounce) container jumbo lump crabmeat, picked through

1 cup shredded Parmesan

Crusty bread and crudité, to serve

1 Place the steam rack in the electric pressure cooker and add the water. Grease a 6-inch round baking dish with cooking spray.

2 Combine the cream cheese, mayonnaise, lemon zest and juice, scallions, mustard, salt, pepper, Old Bay, cayenne, and crabmeat in a large bowl. Transfer to the baking dish, cover with foil, and place in the pressure cooker. Secure the lid and set on Manual with high pressure for 10 minutes. Allow to naturally release for 5 minutes, then quick release.

3 Preheat the oven to broil. Remove the baking dish from the pressure cooker, sprinkle with Parmesan and place in the oven until golden brown and bubbly, 3 to 4 minutes. Remove and serve with crusty bread and crudité.

HOPPIN' JOHN

★ ★ ★

This Southern classic side dish is typically made with black-eyed peas. But you can substitute your favorite beans in this recipe!

2 tablespoons olive oil

3 slices bacon, sliced ½-inch pieces

1 onion, finely chopped

2 carrots, peeled and small diced

2 stalks celery, small diced

1 green bell pepper, stemmed, seeded, and small diced

2 garlic cloves, minced

¼ teaspoon cayenne pepper

1 teaspoon thyme or 2 teaspoons dried thyme

1 teaspoon kosher salt

½ teaspoon freshly ground black pepper

1 pound dried black-eyed peas, rinsed and quick soaked (see note) or soaked overnight

3 cups chicken stock

White rice, cooked, to serve

Scallions, thinly sliced, to garnish

SERVES 4 TO 6

PREP TIME: 15 minutes
COOK TIME: 25 minutes

NOTE

To quick soak peas or beans, rinse them thoroughly and place in the bowl of the pressure cooker with 8 cups of water. Bring to a boil on the Sauté setting. Once boiling, secure the lid and set on Manual with high pressure for 2 minutes. Quick release, drain peas, rinse, and set aside.

1 Select the Sauté setting and heat the olive oil. Add the bacon and cook until browned and crispy, about 6 minutes. Remove to a plate and set aside. Drain half of the fat and discard. Add the onion, carrots, celery, bell pepper, and garlic and cook until almost translucent, about 4 minutes. Add the cayenne, thyme, salt, and pepper and cook an additional minute. Add the black-eyed peas and chicken stock.

2 Secure the lid and place on Manual with high pressure for 15 minutes. Use quick release. Serve over white rice and garnish with scallions.

RED BEANS AND RICE

★ ★ ★

SERVES 4 TO 6
PREP TIME: 15 minutes
COOK TIME: 28 minutes

Imagine tender beans, packed with flavor, served over rice in almost no time! Add your favorite sausage or chicken to this dish to make a complete meal.

2 tablespoons olive oil

8 ounces andouille sausage, sliced ¼-inch thick

1 onion, small diced

3 garlic cloves, minced

1 green bell pepper, stemmed, seeded, and small diced

2 stalks celery, small diced

1 tablespoon paprika

2 teaspoons onion powder

2 teaspoons garlic powder

2 teaspoons dried thyme

2 teaspoons dried oregano

¼ teaspoon cayenne pepper

2 bay leaves

1 pound dried red beans, rinsed, picked through, and quick soaked (see note on page 107) or soaked overnight

1 teaspoon kosher salt

½ teaspoon freshly ground black pepper

4 cups chicken stock

White rice, cooked, to serve

Scallions, thinly sliced, to garnish

1 Select the Sauté setting and heat the olive oil. Add sausage and cook until golden brown on both sides, about 7 minutes. Transfer to a paper towel–lined plate.

2 Add the onion, garlic, bell pepper, and celery and cook until almost translucent, about 4 minutes. Add the paprika, onion powder, garlic powder, thyme, oregano, cayenne, and bay leaves and cook an additional minute. Add the beans and season with salt and pepper. Add the chicken stock.

3 Secure the lid and place on Manual with high pressure for 15 minutes. Use quick release and remove the lid. Remove the bay leaves. Serve over white rice and garnish with scallions.

COLLARD GREENS
WITH BACON

★ ★ ★

This Southern vegetable staple usually takes hours to cook. Using the pressure cooker, you can cook collards every night of the week in about a half hour. Pair with the Spice-Rubbed Roast Chicken (page 81) or other Southern sides to make a complete Southern feast!

2 tablespoons olive oil

5 slices bacon, cut into ½-inch pieces

1 onion, thinly sliced

4 cloves garlic, minced

2 large bunches of collards, stemmed and roughly chopped

1 cup chicken stock

¼ cup apple cider vinegar

2 teaspoons honey

1 teaspoon crushed red pepper flakes

2 teaspoons paprika

1 teaspoon kosher salt

½ teaspoon freshly ground black pepper

Hot sauce (page 131 or store bought), to serve

1 Select the Sauté setting and heat the olive oil. Add the bacon and cook until golden and crispy, about 7 minutes. Transfer to a paper towel–lined plate and set aside. Add onion and garlic and cook until the onion is almost translucent, about 4 minutes. Add the collards in bunches, allowing to wilt slightly. Add the remaining ingredients except the hot sauce.

2 Secure the lid and place on Manual with high pressure for 6 minutes. Allow to naturally release for 5 minutes, then remove the lid. Add the bacon and serve with hot sauce.

SERVES 4 TO 6

PREP TIME: 10 minutes

COOK TIME: 25 minutes

SLOW COOKER
SETTING

Follow the steps below. For step 2, once the lid is secure, select the Slow Cook low setting and cook for 8 to 10 hours or until the collards are tender. Remove the lid, add the bacon back to the pot, and serve.

CLASSIC SOUTHERN CORN BREAD

★ ★ ★

SERVES 4 TO 6
PREP TIME: 10 minutes
COOK TIME: 50 minutes

This is the perfect bread to go with any Southern meal. Use crumbs to top Pimento Macaroni and Cheese (see page 115) or as croutons to finish a salad, and freeze leftovers so that you always have it on hand.

1½ cups water

Cooking spray, to grease

1½ cups cornmeal

½ cup flour

½ cup sugar

2 tablespoons light brown sugar

1 tablespoon baking powder

1 teaspoon kosher salt

3 tablespoons honey

2 large eggs, lightly beaten

¾ cup low-fat buttermilk

½ stick unsalted butter, melted

¾ cup frozen corn, thawed

1 Place the steam rack inside of the pressure cooker and fill with the water. Grease a 7-inch round cake pan with cooking spray. Make a foil strap (see page 9) to easily wrap around the base of the cake pan.

2 Combine the cornmeal, flour, sugar, brown sugar, baking powder, and salt together in a large bowl. In a separate medium bowl combine the honey, eggs, buttermilk, and butter. Add the wet ingredients to the dry, mixing until just combined. Add the corn and mix to combine. Pour into the cake pan and cover with a paper towel and then a piece of foil. Use the foil strap to place the cake pan inside the pressure cooker.

3 Secure the lid and set on Manual with high pressure for 40 minutes. Allow to naturally release for 10 minutes, then quick release and remove the lid. Be sure that an inserted toothpick comes out clean. If the corn bread needs to cook longer, secure

the lid again and place on high pressure for 4 to 5 minutes. Then quick
release, remove the lid, and check with a toothpick again. Allow to cool
in the pan and serve.

PIMENTO MACARONI AND CHEESE

★ ★ ★

No more boxed macaroni and cheese! Believe it or not you can make homemade macaroni and cheese in minutes with your pressure cooker. Pimento Macaroni and Cheese is a great Southern twist on a classic, and it has a nice spicy kick. Add your own favorite cheeses for a changeup.

SERVES 4

PREP TIME: 10 minutes
COOK TIME: 12 minutes

NOTE

Before you make the pasta, you can toast the bread crumbs using the Sauté setting with 1 tablespoon of olive oil or butter until golden brown. Remove the bread crumbs and wipe out the pot before cooking the macaroni and cheese.

1 pound elbow macaroni

3½ cups water

2 tablespoons unsalted butter

1 shallot, peeled and minced

2 teaspoons Dijon mustard

½ teaspoon cayenne pepper

2 teaspoons kosher salt

½ teaspoon freshly ground black pepper

¾ cup reduced fat milk

6 ounces cream cheese, softened

1 cup grated extra sharp Cheddar

1 cup grated Monterey Jack

½ cup pimentos, drained and chopped

¾ cup herbed Panko bread crumbs, toasted, to garnish (optional; see note)

1 Combine the pasta and water in the bowl of the pressure cooker. Secure the lid and place on Manual with high pressure. Cook for 4 minutes, then use quick release to remove the lid. Transfer the pasta to a bowl.

2 Select the Sauté setting and add the butter and shallot and cook until translucent, about 3 minutes. Add the mustard, cayenne pepper, salt, pepper, and milk and whisk to combine. Bring to a simmer and add the cheeses, pimentos, and pasta. Stir to coat the pasta, then divide among bowls and garnish with toasted bread crumbs, if desired.

CREAMED CORN

★ ★ ★

Creamed Corn is the perfect dish for the heart of the summer when the corn is sweet and fresh. You can even make it when corn is in season and freeze it for a side dish that gives you the taste of summer all year long.

2 tablespoons unsalted butter

1 shallot, minced

1 teaspoon thyme leaves or 2 teaspoons dried thyme leaves

10 ears corn, shucked and cut from cob, or 5 cups frozen corn, thawed

1 teaspoon kosher salt

½ teaspoon freshly ground black pepper

¾ cup chicken stock or water

1 tablespoon flour

½ cup whole milk

SERVES 4

PREP TIME: 15 minutes
COOK TIME: 15 minutes

SLOW COOKER
SETTING

After step 1 below, secure the lid and place on the Slow Cook high setting for 1½ to 2 hours or until the corn is almost tender. Return to the Sauté setting and proceed with step 3.

1 Select the Sauté setting on the pressure cooker and add the butter. Add the shallot and thyme and cook for a minute. Add the corn and cook for another 2 minutes; season with salt and pepper. Add the chicken stock.

2 Secure the lid and cook on Manual with high pressure for 8 minutes.

3 Use quick release and return to the Sauté setting. Once simmering, add the flour and milk, stirring to combine. Remove 1 cup of the corn mixture and pulse in a food processor until smooth. Return to the pot and continue to simmer until slightly thickened, another 3 minutes.

BOURBON BROWN SUGAR SWEET POTATO MASH

★ ★ ★

This favorite Thanksgiving side dish can be easily made in your pressure cooker. Adding bourbon takes your potatoes up a notch, Southern-style!

4 sweet potatoes, peeled and medium diced

½ cup water

2 tablespoons unsalted butter

⅓ cup dark brown sugar

½ teaspoon cinnamon

2 tablespoons honey

1 teaspoon kosher salt

½ teaspoon freshly ground black pepper

2 tablespoons bourbon

½ cup toasted pecans, roughly chopped

SERVES 4 TO 6

PREP TIME: 10 minutes
COOK TIME: 10 minutes

SLOW COOKER SETTING

Follow the method below. For step 2, once the lid is secure, select the Slow Cook high setting and cook for 3½ to 4 hours or until the potatoes are tender. Proceed with step 3.

1 Place the sweet potatoes, water, butter, brown sugar, cinnamon, honey, salt, and pepper in the pot of the pressure cooker.

2 Secure the lid and set on Manual with high pressure for 8 minutes.

3 Use the quick release and return to the Sauté setting. Mash the potatoes, add the bourbon, and continue to mash until smooth. Garnish with toasted pecans.

SMOKY SWEET BAKED BEANS

★ ★ ★

The iconic barbecue side is known for its rich molasses flavor with a kick of bacon. You can bring that barbecue flavor to the table any night of the week, as these beans cook in under an hour.

2 tablespoons olive oil

4 slices bacon, cut into ½-inch pieces

1 onion, finely chopped

⅓ cup molasses

½ cup ketchup

¼ cup dark brown sugar

2 teaspoons Dijon mustard

1 teaspoon smoked paprika

¼ teaspoon cayenne

1 teaspoon kosher salt

½ teaspoon freshly ground black pepper

1 pound navy beans, rinsed, picked through, and quick soaked (see note on page 107) or soaked overnight

2 cups chicken stock

SERVES 4 TO 6
PREP TIME: 10 minutes
COOK TIME: 50 minutes

SLOW COOKER
SETTING

Use 4 (15-ounce) cans of navy beans, drained and rinsed. In step 2, use only ¾ cup of chicken stock. For step 3, once the lid is secure, select the Slow Cook low setting and cook for 6 hours or until the flavors are combined. Add the bacon and serve.

1 Select the Sauté setting and heat the olive oil. Add the bacon and cook until golden brown and crispy, about 7 minutes. Remove to a paper towel–lined plate.

2 Add the onion and cook until almost translucent, about 4 minutes. Add the molasses, ketchup, brown sugar, mustard, paprika, cayenne, salt, and pepper. Stir to combine. Add the navy beans and chicken stock.

3 Secure the lid and cook on Manual with high pressure for 30 minutes. Use natural release for 10 minutes, then quick release and remove the lid.

4 Return to the Sauté setting and simmer until thickened, if necessary. Stir in the bacon and serve.

CHEESY POTATOES

★ ★ ★

Cheesy Potatoes is the perfect crowd-pleasing side dish for any party. Make this dish in the electric pressure cooker, bring it to the party, and then place it under a broiler right before serving!

SERVES 4

PREP TIME: 10 minutes
COOK TIME: 32 minutes

- 1½ cups water
- 2 tablespoons unsalted butter, melted, plus additional to grease pan
- ⅔ cup heavy cream
- 1 teaspoon fresh thyme leaves or 2 teaspoons dried thyme
- ½ bunch chives, chopped
- 1 teaspoon kosher salt
- ½ teaspoon freshly ground black pepper
- 2 medium russet potatoes, peeled and sliced ¼-inch thick
- 1½ cups shredded white Cheddar

1 Place the steam rack inside the pot and add the water. Grease a 6-inch baking dish or soufflé dish with butter.

2 Combine the heavy cream, melted butter, thyme, chives, salt, and pepper. Line the potatoes up in the baking dish, stacking on top of each other in a circle. Sprinkle with half of the cheese and pour over half of the cream mixture. Stack a second layer on top. Pour the remaining heavy cream mixture over the top and cover with foil. Place the baking dish on top of the steamer rack.

3 Secure the lid and cook on Manual with high pressure for 24 minutes. Allow to naturally release for 5 minutes, then quick release and remove the lid.

4 Preheat the broiler. Place the baking dish on a baking sheet and sprinkle with the remaining cheese. Place under the broiler and allow to cook for 2 to 3 minutes, or until cheese has melted and is golden brown.

CORN BREAD DRESSING

★ ★ ★

SERVES 4 TO 6
PREP TIME: 15 minutes
COOK TIME: 20 minutes

This is the perfect side dish for using up leftover corn bread and vegetables. Pair it with chicken or turkey for a complete Sunday supper.

1½ cups water

3 tablespoons unsalted butter, divided

1 small onion, small diced

2 stalks celery, small diced

2 carrots, peeled and small diced

2 garlic cloves, minced

½ teaspoon fresh thyme or 1 teaspoon dried thyme

1 teaspoon fresh sage, chopped, or 2 teaspoons dried sage

2 tablespoons parsley, chopped

1 teaspoon kosher salt

½ teaspoon freshly ground black pepper

5 cups 1-inch-cubed Classic Southern Corn Bread (see page 112) or store bought

⅔ cup chicken stock

1 Place the steam rack in the pressure cooker and add the water. Grease a 6-inch round baking dish or soufflé dish with 1 tablespoon of butter.

2 Heat a medium sauté pan over medium-high heat and add remaining 2 tablespoons of the butter. Add the onion, celery, carrots, and garlic and cook until almost translucent, about 4 minutes. Add the thyme, sage, parsley, salt, and pepper and cook an additional minute. Transfer to a large bowl, add the corn bread and the stock and toss to combine.

3 Transfer to the baking dish and allow to rest for 5 minutes. Place a piece of paper towel, then a piece of foil on top of the baking dish and place on top of the steam rack. Secure the lid and place on Manual with high pressure for 10 minutes. Allow to naturally release for 5 minutes, then quick release and remove the lid.

 If desired, preheat the oven to 400°F. Place the baking dish in the oven to toast the dressing on the top, about 5 minutes.

BRAISED CABBAGE

★ ★ ★

While braised cabbage is typically considered a side dish, it can also be a perfect vegetarian entrée. Use your favorite spices, herbs, or even pesto for variations on this dish.

SERVES 4 TO 6 AS A SIDE DISH,
4 AS A MAIN DISH

PREP TIME: 5 minutes
COOK TIME: 28 minutes

2 tablespoons olive oil

1 shallot, thinly sliced

2 garlic cloves, minced

1 head green cabbage, core removed and thinly sliced

1 teaspoon kosher salt

½ teaspoon freshly ground black pepper

1 teaspoon paprika

1 teaspoon dried oregano

¼ teaspoon cayenne pepper

½ cup vegetable stock

⅓ cup apple cider vinegar

SLOW COOKER
SETTING

Follow the instructions below. When the lid is secure, select the Slow Cook low setting and cook for 4 to 6 hours or until the cabbage is tender and cooked through.

1 Select the Sauté setting and heat the olive oil. Add the shallot and garlic and cook until almost translucent, about 3 minutes. Add the cabbage in batches and allow to slightly wilt, 10 to 12 minutes. Season with salt, pepper, paprika, oregano, and cayenne. Add the stock and vinegar.

2 Secure the lid, and set on Manual with high pressure for 8 minutes. Allow to naturally release for 5 minutes, then quick release and remove the lid.

★ ★ ★

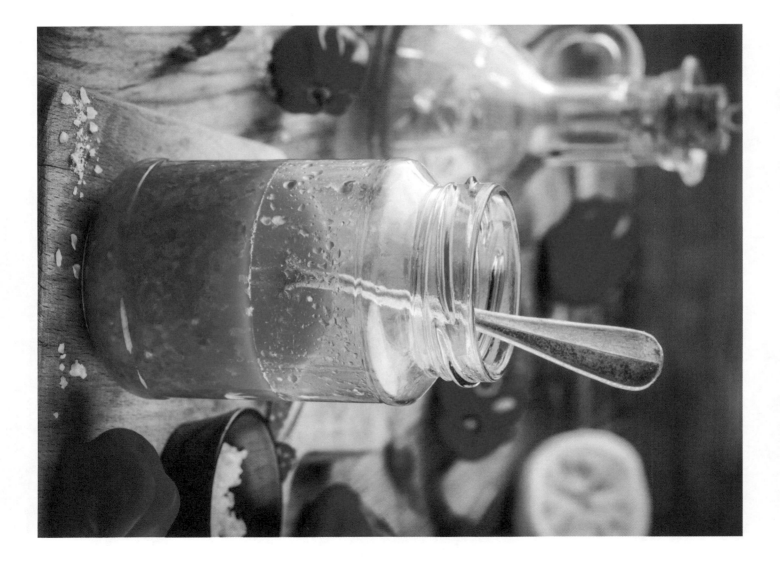

HOT SAUCE

★ ★ ★

Kick up the heat in under 10 minutes using your pressure cooker! Choose your favorite spicy chilies to customize your hot sauce.

YIELDS 3 CUPS

PREP TIME: 5 minutes
COOK TIME: 2 minutes
+ cooling time

NOTE

This hot sauce can be stored for up to 2 weeks in the refrigerator. For a longer preserved hot sauce, follow canning procedures outlined by the FDA.

---

3 cups Fresno chili peppers or cherry peppers, stemmed

1 habanero pepper, stemmed

2 red bell peppers, stemmed and seeded

2 cloves garlic

¾ cup apple cider vinegar

¼ cup water

1 teaspoon sea salt

Sterilized heatproof jars, boiled in water for 10 minutes

1 Add the peppers and garlic to the bowl of a food processor and pulse until finely chopped. Transfer to the bowl of the pressure cooker and add the cider vinegar, water, and sea salt.

2 Secure the lid and place on Manual with high pressure for 2 minutes. Use quick release and remove the sauce to a container to cool completely without the lid.

3 If you prefer a smooth hot sauce, return the hot sauce to the food processor or blender and purée until smooth. Transfer to sterilized jars and cool completely without the lids. Once cool, secure the lids and store in the refrigerator for up to 2 weeks (see note).

APPLESAUCE

★ ★ ★

This childhood classic is the perfect snack or side dish to any meal. Use your favorite apples when making this applesauce. It is delicious served with Sweet Tea Pork Tenderloin (page 52) or Pulled Pork (page 44).

SERVES 8 TO 10
PREP TIME: 15 minutes
COOK TIME: 10 minutes

12 apples of your choosing, peeled, cored, and large diced

¼ cup water

½ cup dark brown sugar

1 lemon, zested and juiced

1 teaspoon kosher salt

1 teaspoon cinnamon

1 Combine all the ingredients in the bowl of the pressure cooker. Secure the lid and cook on Manual with high pressure for 5 minutes. Allow to naturally release for 5 minutes, then quick release and remove lid.

2 Set pressure cooker to the Sauté setting and simmer until thickened if necessary. Mash the applesauce using a wooden spoon or a handheld mixer to the desired consistency. Serve warm, at room temperature, or chilled.

CRANBERRY APPLE RAISIN CHUTNEY

★ ★ ★

This chutney is the perfect condiment for meats or even a sandwich! Use this recipe year round with your favorite fruits for a delicious pop of flavor to accompany any dish.

1 shallot, minced

¾ cup dark brown sugar

2 tablespoons honey

½ orange, zested and juiced

⅔ cup apple cider vinegar

1 teaspoon cinnamon

½ teaspoon ground ginger

¼ teaspoon ground cloves

1 teaspoon kosher salt

¾ cup golden raisins

3 apples of your choice, peeled, cored, and cut into ½-inch dice

1 (10-ounce) bag frozen cranberries, thawed

Sterilized heatproof jars, boiled in water for 10 minutes

SERVES 15 TO 20

PREP TIME: 15 minutes
COOK TIME: 17 minutes + cooling time

SLOW COOKER SETTING

Follow the method below. For step 2, after securing the lid, set on the Slow Cook low setting for 3 hours or until thickened.

NOTE

This chutney can be stored for up to 2 weeks in the refrigerator. For a longer preserved chutney, follow canning procedures outlined by the FDA.

1 Add the shallot, brown sugar, honey, orange zest and juice, vinegar, cinnamon, ginger, cloves, salt, and raisins to the pressure cooker and bring to a simmer on the Sauté setting. Once simmering, add the apples and cranberries.

2 Secure the lid and set on Manual with high pressure for 7 minutes. Allow to naturally release for 5 minutes, then quick release and remove lid.

3 Return to the Sauté setting to thicken if necessary. Transfer to sterilized jars, allow to cool completely without the lids, then serve or secure the lids and store in the refrigerator for up to 2 weeks (see note).

SPICY AND SWEET BARBECUE SAUCE

★ ★ ★

YIELDS 2½ CUPS

PREP TIME: 5 minutes
COOK TIME: 23 minutes

Forget buying barbecue sauce from the store—make your own in just minutes. You will want to make extra because it will run out quickly! Freeze any extra sauce and thaw when ready to use.

2 tablespoons olive oil

1 small red onion, small diced

2 garlic cloves, minced

1 jalapeño, seeded and minced

1 teaspoon crushed red pepper flakes

1½ cups ketchup

1 cup tomato purée

¾ cup dark brown sugar

⅓ cup honey

⅔ cup apple cider vinegar

½ cup water

2 tablespoons Worcestershire sauce

1 tablespoon Dijon mustard

1 teaspoon kosher salt

2 teaspoons freshly ground black pepper

1 Select the Sauté setting and heat the olive oil. Add the onion, garlic, and jalapeño and sauté until almost tender, about 5 minutes. Add the crushed red pepper flakes during the last minute of cooking. Turn the Sauté setting off and add the remaining ingredients. Secure the lid and set on Manual with low pressure for 12 minutes. Allow to naturally release for 5 minutes, then quick release and remove the lid.

2 Allow to cool completely and use as a condiment or in your favorite recipes! Barbecue sauce can be stored in the refrigerator for up to 1 week or in the freezer for up to 3 months.

CHICKEN STOCK

★ ★ ★

Homemade stock can make any recipe that much richer, but stock is a hassle to make using traditional methods and requires hours of work at the stove. A pressure cooker changes all of that. Make large batches of this quick chicken stock in advance and then freeze for easy weeknight meal preparations.

YIELDS 9 CUPS

PREP TIME: 5 minutes
COOK TIME: 1 hour 15 minutes
+ cooling time

———◆———

TIP

Use the boiled chicken in another dish!

1 chicken, broken down into 8 pieces or roasted chicken bones

1 small onion, halved

1 carrot, peeled and cut into large pieces

1 stalk celery, cut into large pieces

2 cloves garlic, peeled

2 teaspoons black peppercorns

3 sprigs fresh thyme

1 Place all the ingredients in the bowl of the pressure cooker and cover with water, about 8 to 9 cups. Secure the lid and set on Manual with high pressure for 50 minutes. Allow to naturally release.

2 Strain the broth and allow to cool completely. Store in the refrigerator for up to 1 week or freeze for up to 3 months.

BEEF STOCK

★ ★ ★

YIELDS 9 CUPS

PREP TIME: 15 minutes
COOK TIME: 1 hour 20 minutes
+ cooling time

This beef stock adds a flavor that is rich and flavorful to any recipe. Try using in the Sweet and Spicy Braised Beef Brisket recipe (see page 48) or Sunday Pot Roast (see page 56).

2 tablespoons olive oil

2–3 pounds beef bones

1 small onion, quartered

1 carrot, peeled and cut into large pieces

1 stalk celery, cut into large pieces

2 cloves garlic, peeled

3 sprigs thyme

2 teaspoons black peppercorns

1 Preheat the oven to 450°F. Line a baking sheet with foil.

2 Place the bones on the baking sheet. Toss with the olive oil and place in the oven to roast for 20 minutes. Remove and allow to cool.

3 Add the bones and the remaining ingredients to the bowl of the pressure cooker and cover with water, about 8 to 9 cups. Secure the lid and place on Manual with high pressure for 45 minutes. Allow to naturally release.

4 Strain the stock through a fine mesh sieve and allow to cool to room temperature. Once the stock cools, skim off and remove excess fat. Refrigerate for up to 1 week or freeze for up to 3 months until ready to use.

SPICY PICKLES

★ ★ ★

Spicy Pickles are the perfect condiment for any lunch sandwich or cookout. With a pressure cooker you can make pickles in minutes. Use this quick pickle recipe for any of your favorite summer vegetables—not just cucumbers!

YIELDS 5 TO 6 CUPS

PREP TIME: 5 minutes
COOK TIME: 6 minutes
+ cooling time

NOTE

This is a quick pickle. Store pickles in the refrigerator for up to 2 weeks. If you desire canned pickles, follow canning procedures outlined by the FDA.

2 English cucumbers, sliced ¼-inch thick

1½ cups apple cider vinegar

⅔ cup water

2 tablespoons sugar

1 teaspoon kosher salt

2 teaspoons red chili flakes

2 cloves garlic, crushed

1 teaspoon black peppercorns

Sterilized heatproof jars, boiled in water for 10 minutes

1 Place all the food ingredients in the bowl of the pressure cooker. Secure the lid and place on Manual with high pressure for 1 minute. Allow to naturally release for 5 minutes, then quick release and remove the lid.

2 Remove the pickles and pickling liquid to the jars until they are three-quarters of the way full. Secure the lids and allow to cool to room temperature before serving or refrigerating (see note).

PEACH PEPPER JELLY

★ ★ ★

Peaches in this classic pepper jelly spread provide a sweetness that perfectly accompanies cheese or meat. Jar this jelly to make the perfect gift!

3 yellow bell peppers, stemmed, seeded, and roughly chopped

3 peaches, peeled, stone removed, and roughly chopped

3 jalapeño peppers, stemmed, seeded, and roughly chopped

⅔ cup apple cider vinegar

2½ cups sugar

1½ tablespoons pectin or according to box directions

Sterilized heatproof jars, boiled in water for 10 minutes

YIELDS 3 CUPS

PREP TIME: 20 minutes
COOK TIME: 10 minutes
+ cooling time

NOTE

This pepper jelly can be stored for up to 2 weeks in the refrigerator. For a longer preserved pepper jelly, follow canning procedures outlined by the FDA.

1 Place the bell peppers, peaches, and jalapeños in the bowl of a food processor and pulse until finely chopped. Transfer to the bowl of the pressure cooker and add the apple cider vinegar and sugar. Secure the lid and place on Manual with high pressure for 3 minutes. Allow to naturally release for 5 minutes, then quick release and remove the lid.

2 Set the pressure cooker to the Sauté setting and bring to a boil. Stir in the pectin and boil for 1 minute. Remove the metal bowl from the pressure cooker and skim off any foam from the surface. Fill the sterilized jars until three-quarters full and seal with lid. Allow to cool to room temperature, then store in the refrigerator (see note).

ORANGE MARMALADE

★ ★ ★

Perfect for breakfast or a snack, orange marmalade is the ultimate citrus spread on biscuits or toast. Make this marmalade as a gift or bring it to brunch at a friend's house—everyone will love it!

YIELDS 5 CUPS

PREP TIME: 20 minutes
COOK TIME: 20 minutes
+ cooling time

NOTE

Store the marmalade in the refrigerator for up to 2 weeks. If you prefer a longer canning shelf life, follow the canning procedures outlined by the FDA.

2 pounds navel oranges, about 6 oranges

½ cup water

1 cup sugar

3 teaspoons lemon juice

1½ tablespoons fruit pectin or according to package directions

Sterilized heatproof jars, boiled in water for 10 minutes

1. Peel the oranges and thinly slice the peels. Segment the oranges by slicing wedges into the orange using a paring knife between the membranes. Cut the orange segments in half. Place the orange peels, segments, and juice of the membranes into the bowl of the pressure cooker. Add the water and place on Manual with high pressure for 10 minutes. Allow to naturally release for 5 minutes, then quick release and remove the lid.

2. Set the pressure cooker to the Sauté setting. Bring to a simmer, stir in the sugar and lemon juice, and allow the sugar to dissolve and the marmalade to thicken, 3 to 4 minutes. Add the fruit pectin during the last minute of boiling and stir vigorously to combine.

3. Turn the pressure cooker off and transfer the marmalade to the sterilized jars, filling the jars three-quarters full. Allow to cool to room temperature without the lids, then seal and store in the refrigerator (see note).

HONEY TOMATO JAM

★ ★ ★

This classic Southern condiment is a must-have addition to a cheese board. Make this jam when tomatoes are ripe and freeze it in batches to enjoy throughout the year.

6 large tomatoes, stems removed

2 tablespoons olive oil

1 shallot, minced

¾ cup dark brown sugar

2 tablespoons honey

1 lemon, zested and juiced

2 teaspoons kosher salt

½ teaspoon freshly ground black pepper

Sterilized heatproof jars, boiled in water for 10 minutes

YIELDS 2 CUPS

PREP TIME: 20 minutes
COOK TIME: 35 minutes
+cooling time

NOTE

Store this jam in the refrigerator for up to 2 weeks. If you prefer a longer canning shelf life, follow canning procedures outlined by the FDA.

1 Bring a large saucepan of water to a boil. Make an X on the bottom of each tomato and place in the boiling water for 1–2 minutes. Remove and run under cold water until cooled. Peel the skin off the tomatoes. Slice the tomatoes in half and squeeze to remove the seeds. Chop the tomatoes into ½-inch pieces. Set aside.

2 Select the Sauté setting on the pressure cooker and heat the olive oil. Add the shallot and cook until almost translucent, about 4 minutes. Add the remaining ingredients to the pressure cooker, secure the lid, and place on Manual with high pressure for 10 minutes. Allow to naturally release for 5 minutes, then quick release and remove the lid.

3 Return to the Sauté setting and simmer until thickened, about 10 minutes. Transfer to the sterilized jars, fill three-quarters of the way full, and allow to cool completely before serving or storing (see note).

BOURBON CARAMEL SAUCE

★ ★ ★

This sauce is perfect for any dessert. From ice cream to cake, just drizzle it on top to add another level of decadence that everyone will love.

YIELDS ABOUT 1 CUP
PREP TIME: 2 minutes
COOK TIME: 6 minutes

1¼ cups brown sugar

½ stick unsalted butter

¾ cup heavy cream

½ teaspoon kosher salt

½ teaspoon vanilla extract

1 tablespoon bourbon

1 Select the Sauté setting on the pressure cooker. Add the brown sugar and butter and stir until combined and melted. Cook for 2 minutes on Sauté. Add the heavy cream and salt, secure the lid, and cook on Manual with high pressure for 4 minutes. Use quick release, then stir in the vanilla extract and bourbon.

2 Allow to cool and remove to a container with an airtight lid. Store in the refrigerator for up to 2 weeks.

LEMON JAM

★ ★ ★

This jam delivers the perfect combination of sweet and tart at the same time, and it makes for a delightful tea time with shortbread cookies or biscuits!

YIELDS 2 CUPS

PREP TIME: 20 minutes
COOK TIME: 20 minutes
+ cooling time

NOTE

Store this jam in the refrigerator for up to 2 weeks. If you prefer a longer canning shelf life, follow canning procedures outlined by the FDA.

10 lemons

½ cup water

1 cup sugar

Sterilized heatproof jars, boiled in water for 10 minutes

1 Peel the lemons and thinly slice the peels. Segment the lemons by slicing wedges into the lemons using a paring knife between the membranes. Cut the lemon segments in half. Place the lemon peels, segments, and juice of the membranes into the bowl of the pressure cooker. Add the water and place on Manual with high pressure for 10 minutes. Allow to naturally release for 5 minutes, then quick release and remove the lid.

2 Set the pressure cooker to the Sauté setting and bring to a simmer. Add the sugar and stir to combine until dissolved. Simmer until thickened, about 5 minutes.

3 Transfer the mixture to a blender and blend until smooth.

4 Transfer to sterilized jars until three-quarters of the way full. Allow to cool completely before serving or storing (see note).

DESSERTS

★ ★ ★

RUM RAISIN
BREAD PUDDING

★ ★ ★

Use your favorite dried or fresh fruits in this bread pudding. It's the perfect warm, sweet dessert for a cold winter night. Serve with ice cream or caramel sauce.

1½ cups water

1 tablespoon unsalted butter, to grease

3 tablespoons unsalted butter, melted

⅓ cup dark brown sugar

2 tablespoons honey

3 large eggs, beaten

½ cup low-fat milk

1 teaspoon kosher salt

1 teaspoon vanilla extract

½ teaspoon cinnamon

¼ teaspoon ground nutmeg

2 tablespoons rum

½ cup raisins

5 cups ½-inch-cubed day-old bread

Ice cream or caramel sauce, to serve (optional)

Chopped nuts, for garnish (optional)

SERVES 4

PREP TIME: 20 minutes
COOK TIME: 25 minutes

SLOW COOKER
SETTING

Follow the method below, adding an extra ½ cup of milk to the mixture in step 2. For step 3, secure the lid and select the Slow Cook normal setting and cook for 2½ to 3 hours or until an inserted toothpick comes out clean. Proceed with step 4.

1 Place the steam rack inside the pressure cooker and add the water. Grease a 6-inch round cake pan with 1 tablespoon of butter.

2 Combine the remaining ingredients in a large bowl. Transfer to the cake pan and allow to sit for 10 minutes. Cover with a paper towel, then a piece of foil. Make a foil strap (see page 9) to go around the cake pan and place on the steamer rack.

3 Secure the lid and place on Manual with high pressure for 10 minutes. Allow to naturally release for 10 minutes, then quick release and remove the lid.

4 If desired, preheat the oven to 400°F. Place the bread pudding in the oven to toast the top cubes of bread, about 4 minutes. Serve with ice cream or caramel sauce and chopped nuts, if using.

PECAN PRALINE CHEESECAKE

★ ★ ★

SERVES 6
PREP TIME: 20 minutes
COOK TIME: 50 minutes
+ 4 hours in refrigerator

Forget the hassle of making cheesecake in the oven. The pressure cooker keeps cheesecake moist, and this worry-free recipe is easy to make. Make this dessert well in advance, because it needs to chill in the refrigerator before serving.

FOR THE CRUST

Cooking spray, to grease

1½ cups water

1½ cups graham cracker crumbs

3 tablespoons unsalted butter, melted

1 tablespoon honey

½ teaspoon kosher salt

½ cup toasted pecans, finely chopped

FOR THE FILLING

2 (8-ounce) blocks cream cheese, softened

⅓ cup dark brown sugar

¼ cup sugar

⅓ cup sour cream

1 teaspoon vanilla extract

1 teaspoon kosher salt

1 teaspoon cinnamon

¼ teaspoon nutmeg

1 tablespoon flour

2 large eggs

1 large egg yolk, lightly beaten

1 cup Bourbon Caramel Sauce (see page 151) or store bought

1 cup toasted pecans, to garnish

1 MAKE THE CRUST Preheat the oven to 350°F. Grease an 8-inch springform pan with cooking spray. Wrap the bottom of the pan with foil to prevent the cheesecake batter from leaking. Place the steam rack in the bottom of the pot and fill with the water.

continued

2 In a large bowl, add the graham cracker crumbs, butter, honey, and salt and mix until the crust just comes together. Transfer to the pan and press down to form a crust. Place in the oven and bake until golden brown, 10 to 12 minutes. Allow to cool completely. Sprinkle the pecans over the cooled crust.

3 **MAKE THE FILLING** Place the cream cheese in a large bowl and beat until smooth using a handheld mixer or in the bowl of a stand mixer fitted with the paddle attachment. Add the brown sugar and sugar and mix until light and fluffy. Add the sour cream and mix until just combined. Add the vanilla, salt, cinnamon, nutmeg, and flour and mix until just combined. Add the eggs and egg yolk, one at a time, mixing until just incorporated; do not overmix. Transfer the batter to the springform pan and smooth the top. Place a piece of paper towel and foil on top of the pan.

4 Make a foil strap (see page 9) to wrap around the bottom of the pan and place in the pressure cooker. Secure the lid and place on Manual with high pressure for 27 minutes. Allow to naturally release, then remove the lid.

5 Remove the cheesecake from the pressure cooker, be sure that there is just a slight jiggle in the center, and allow to cool to room temperature. If the cheesecake still has a runny center, secure the lid again on the pressure cooker and select Manual with high pressure for another 4 minutes and check again. Run a knife around the edge of the pan, cover the pan, and place in the refrigerator to chill for at least 4 hours or overnight.

6 To serve, remove the cheesecake from the pan; pour the caramel sauce all over the top of the cheesecake and top with toasted pecans.

COCONUT CREAM PIE

★ ★ ★

Bring tropical paradise to your home! This coconut custard pie is the perfect complement to any summer dinner and can be made in advance. Try adding lime juice or other tropical fruit flavors to this pie.

SERVES 6
PREP TIME: 25 minutes
COOK TIME: 50 minutes
+ 2 hours in refrigerator

FOR THE CRUST

Cooking spray, to grease

1½ cups water

1½ cups graham cracker crumbs

3 tablespoons unsalted butter, melted

1 tablespoon honey

½ teaspoon kosher salt

FOR THE CUSTARD

1 (14-ounce) can sweetened condensed milk

½ cup whole milk

2 eggs, beaten

2 egg yolks

2 tablespoons coconut extract

TO SERVE

1 cup heavy whipping cream, chilled

1 teaspoon vanilla extract

2 tablespoons confectioners' sugar

1 cup sweetened coconut, to serve

1 **MAKE THE CRUST** Preheat the oven to 350°F. Grease an 8-inch springform pan with cooking spray. Wrap the bottom of the pan with foil to prevent the filling from leaking. Place the steam rack in the bottom of the pot and add the water.

2 Combine the graham cracker crumbs, butter, honey, and salt in a large bowl. Transfer to the pan and press down to form a crust. Place in the oven and bake until golden brown, about 10 to 12 minutes. Allow to cool completely.

3 **MAKE THE CUSTARD** Combine all the custard ingredients in a large bowl and whisk together until well combined; do not over-mix. Pour into the springform pan, cover with a paper towel and a piece of foil and place on top of the rack with a foil strap (see page 9) around the bottom.

4 Secure the lid and place on Manual with high pressure for 22 minutes. Allow to naturally release for 10 minutes, then remove lid. Remove from the pressure cooker, being sure there is still a slight jiggle in the center of the custard. If the custard is still runny in the center, secure the lid again on the pressure cooker and select Manual with high pressure for another 4 minutes and check again. Allow to cool to room temperature, then run a knife around the edge, cover the pan, and chill in the refrigerator in the pan for at least 2 hours.

5 **TO SERVE** Whip the heavy cream in a large bowl using a handheld mixer or in the bowl of a stand mixer fitted with a whisk attachment. Add the vanilla and the confectioners' sugar and whip until soft-medium peaks form.

6 Toast the coconut in a dry pan over medium-low heat until golden brown, about 5 minutes, stirring throughout.

7 Remove the pie from the pan and top with whipped cream and toasted coconut.

SWEET POTATO PIE

★ ★ ★

This sister to pumpkin pie is great all year round. It is sure to become a family favorite.

SERVES 6

PREP TIME: 25 minutes
COOK TIME: 50 minutes
+ 4 hours in refrigerator

FOR THE CRUST

Cooking spray, to grease

1½ cups water

1½ cups finely ground gingersnaps

1 teaspoon salt

3 tablespoons unsalted butter, melted

FOR THE FILLING

1½ cups cooked, mashed sweet potatoes

¼ cup dark brown sugar

¼ cup sugar

1 tablespoon honey

1 teaspoon vanilla extract

1 teaspoon kosher salt

¾ teaspoon cinnamon

¼ teaspoon nutmeg

¼ teaspoon ground ginger

1 egg, lightly beaten

½ cup evaporated milk

TO SERVE

1 cup heavy whipping cream, chilled

½ teaspoon vanilla extract

2 tablespoons confectioners' sugar

Sliced almonds (optional)

1 MAKE THE CRUST Preheat the oven to 350°F. Grease an 8-inch springform pan with cooking spray. Wrap the bottom of the pan with foil to prevent the filling from leaking. Place the steam rack inside of the pressure cooker and add the water.

2 Combine the gingersnaps, salt, and butter in a large bowl. Transfer to the pan and press down to form an even crust. Bake in the oven until golden brown, about 10 to 12 minutes. Remove from the oven and allow to cool completely.

3 MAKE THE FILLING Combine all the filling ingredients in a large bowl and whisk until just combined. Pour into the pan and smooth the top. Cover with a paper towel and then a piece of

continued

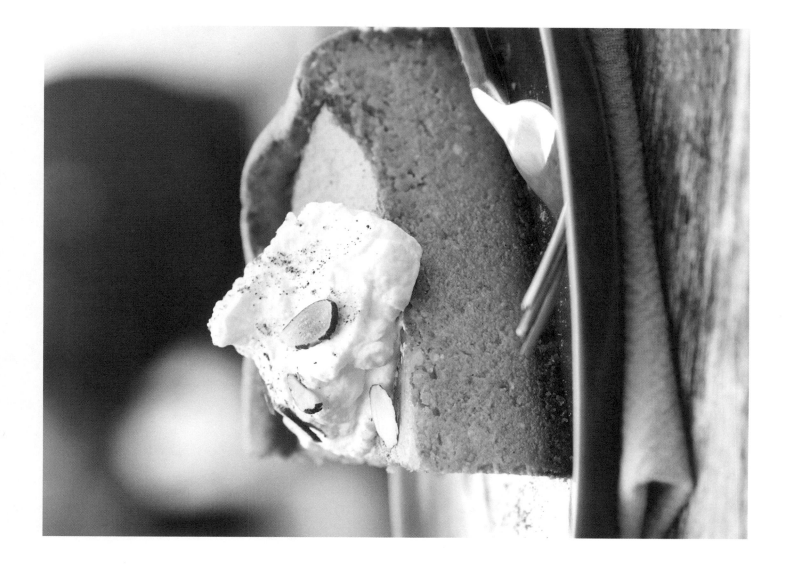

foil. Secure a foil strap (see page 9) around the bottom of the cake pan then place on the steam rack. Secure the lid and place on Manual with high pressure for 30 minutes. Allow to naturally release then remove from the pot. Allow to cool to room temperature, run a knife around the edge of the pan, cover the pan, and chill in the refrigerator for 4 hours.

4 **TO SERVE** Whip the heavy cream in a large bowl using a hand-held mixer or in the bowl of a stand mixer fitted with a whisk attachment. Add the vanilla and the confectioners' sugar and whip until soft-medium peaks form.

5 Serve the pie with whipped cream and sliced almonds, if desired.

CINNAMON ROLL PULL-APART BREAD

★ ★ ★

A classic treat that is delicious morning, noon, and night, this pull-apart bread tastes just like cinnamon rolls but without the hassle! Perfect for entertaining.

SERVES 4 TO 6

PREP TIME: 15 minutes
COOK TIME: 20 minutes

FOR THE PULL-APART BREAD

1½ cups water

Cooking spray, to grease

2 large eggs, beaten

½ cup whole milk

1 teaspoon vanilla extract

3 tablespoons unsalted butter, melted

2 teaspoons cinnamon

¾ cup sugar

½ teaspoon kosher salt

1 loaf day-old sliced white bread, each piece cut into 2 rectangles with crust removed

FOR THE GLAZE

1 cup confectioners' sugar

2 tablespoons whole milk

1 **MAKE THE PULL-APART BREAD** Place the steam rack inside of the pressure cooker and add the water. Grease two 5½ × 3-inch mini loaf pans with cooking spray (if you don't have a mini loaf pan you can use a 6-inch round cake pan and line the pieces of bread up in a circular fashion).

2 Add all the roll ingredients except the bread to a baking dish and whisk to combine. Dredge both sides of each bread slice in the egg mixture, then line the pan with the pieces of bread standing upright, starting from the shorter end of the loaf pan. Repeat with the remaining bread until both loaf pans are filled with upright slices of bread. Cover the pans with a piece of paper towel and then a piece of foil. Place the pans on the steam rack.

3 Secure the lid and place on Manual with high pressure for 10 minutes. Allow to naturally release for 5 minutes, then quick release and remove the lid.

continued

4 If desired, preheat the oven to 400°F. Place the bread in the oven to toast the top of the bread for 4 to 5 minutes. Allow to cool for 10 minutes.

5 **MAKE THE GLAZE** In a small bowl whisk the confectioners' sugar and milk together until smooth. Add more milk if a thinner consistency is desired.

6 Remove the loaves from the pans, drizzle with glaze, and serve.

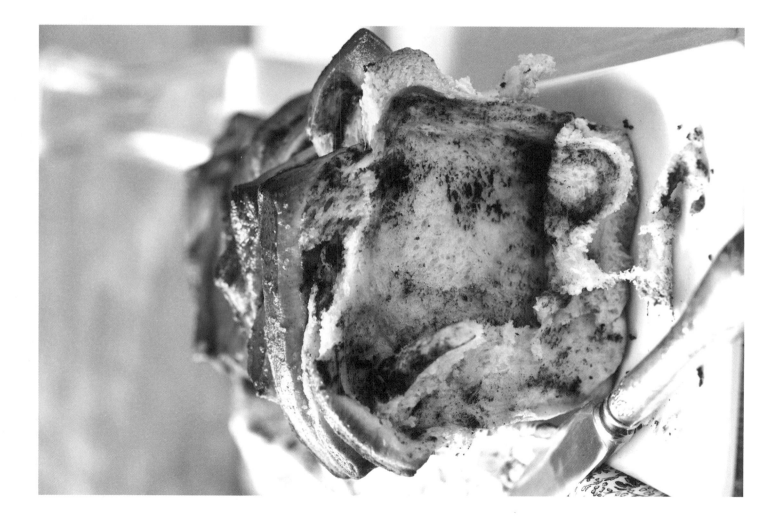

BUTTERSCOTCH PECAN MONKEY BREAD

★ ★ ★

This is the perfect dessert recipe for a weeknight or even a special-occasion brunch. It is so easy you will never have to stress over entertaining. Add mini chocolate chips to make it even more decadent!

SERVES 6 TO 8

PREP TIME: 15 minutes
COOK TIME: 20 minutes

SLOW COOKER
SETTING

Follow the method below. For step 4, once the lid is secure, place on the Slow Cook low setting and cook for 2 to 2½ hours or until the bread is cooked through. Allow to cool in the pan for 5 to 10 minutes, then flip out onto a platter and serve.

1½ cups water

Cooking spray, to grease

2 large eggs

½ cup whole milk

5 cups ½-inch-cubed day-old white bread

½ package butterscotch pudding mix

½ teaspoon cinnamon

½ teaspoon kosher salt

2 tablespoons light brown sugar

½ cup pecans, roughly chopped

½ stick unsalted butter, melted and divided

1 Place the steam rack inside of the pressure cooker and add the water. Grease a 6-inch round cake pan or 6-inch Bundt pan with cooking spray.

2 Add the eggs and milk to a large bowl and whisk to combine. Add the bread and stir to coat. In a separate medium bowl add the pudding mix, cinnamon, salt, brown sugar, and pecans and mix to combine.

3 Add half of the bread mixture to the cake pan. Drizzle with half of the melted butter and sprinkle with half of the pudding mixture. Repeat, ending with the pudding mixture. Cover with a piece of paper towel and a piece of foil. Make a foil strap (see page 9) around the base of the pan and place on top of the steam rack.

4 Secure the lid and cook on Manual with high pressure for 20 minutes. Allow to naturally release for 10 minutes, then quick release and remove the lid.

5 Remove the pan from the pressure cooker and allow to cool in the pan for another 5 to 10 minutes. Flip the monkey bread out onto a platter and serve.

HUMMINGBIRD CAKE

★ ★ ★

SERVES 6 TO 8
PREP TIME: 35 minutes
COOK TIME: 1 hour

Wow your guests with a cake made in the pressure cooker! The classic Southern pineapple-banana cake is sure to be a crowd pleaser. You can use a store-bought cream cheese frosting to prepare the dessert even faster!

FOR THE CAKE

1½ cups water

1 stick plus 1 tablespoon unsalted butter, softened and divided

1¾ cups flour, divided

1 teaspoon baking soda

½ teaspoon kosher salt

½ teaspoon cinnamon

¼ teaspoon ground nutmeg

¼ cup light brown sugar

¾ cup sugar

2 large eggs

2 ripe bananas, peeled and mashed

1 teaspoon vanilla extract

1 (4-ounce) can crushed pineapple in juice, drained

½ cup pecans, roughly chopped

FOR THE FROSTING

1 (8-ounce) package cream cheese, softened

6 tablespoons unsalted butter, softened

1 teaspoon vanilla extract

2¼ cups confectioners' sugar

1–2 tablespoons milk, if needed

1 cup chopped pecans and 12 whole pecans, to garnish (optional)

1 MAKE THE CAKE Place the steam rack inside of the pressure cooker and fill with the water. Grease a 7-inch round cake pan with 1 tablespoon of the butter and dust with ¼ cup of the flour.

continued

2 Combine the remaining 1½ cups flour, baking soda, salt, cinnamon, and nutmeg in a large bowl. In a separate large bowl combine the remaining 1 stick butter with the brown sugar and sugar using a handheld mixer or in the bowl of a stand mixer fitted with a paddle attachment. Beat the butter and sugars on medium speed until light and fluffy, about 4 minutes. Add the eggs, one at a time, being sure to incorporate after each addition. Add the bananas and the vanilla and mix until combined. Add the pineapple and mix until combined. Add the flour mixture in batches, mixing to combine. Remove from the stand mixer if using, add the pecans, and fold to incorporate.

3 Transfer the batter to the cake pan. Cover with a piece of paper towel and a piece of foil. Make a foil strap (see page 9) to wrap around the base of the cake pan. Place the cake pan inside of the pressure cooker, secure the lid, and place on Manual with high pressure for 50 minutes. Allow to naturally release for 10 minutes, then quick release and remove the lid.

4 Remove the cake and allow to cool in the pan for 10 minutes, then remove from the pan and allow to cool completely.

5 **MAKE THE FROSTING** Combine the cream cheese and butter using a handheld mixer or in the bowl of a stand mixer using the paddle attachment. Whip on medium speed until light and fluffy, about 4 minutes. Add the vanilla and mix to combine. Add the confectioners' sugar in stages and continue mixing until combined and the frosting is light and fluffy. If your frosting becomes too thick, add 1 to 2 tablespoons of milk to thin it out.

6 Cut the cake in half horizontally, to create two layers of cake. Spread a layer of frosting in the center. Frost the outside of the cake with a thin layer of frosting. Garnish with whole pecans on top of the cake and chopped pecans around the base, if desired, and serve.

KEY LIME PIE

★ ★ ★

The rich sweetness of the custard filling mixed with the tang of lime juice creates the signature flavor of a key lime pie. Perfect on a summer day, this pie can be frozen and thawed in advance so you always have a last-minute dessert that's ready to serve.

SERVES 6 TO 8
PREP TIME: 30 minutes
COOK TIME: 37 minutes
+ 4 hours in the refrigerator

FOR THE CRUST

1½ cups water

Cooking spray, to grease

1½ cups graham cracker crumbs

3 tablespoons unsalted butter, melted

2 tablespoons dark brown sugar

½ teaspoon kosher salt

FOR THE FILLING

1 (14-ounce) can sweetened condensed milk

2 large eggs, lightly beaten

2 egg yolks

Zest of 2–3 key limes or limes

⅔ cup key lime juice

FOR THE WHIPPED CREAM

½ cup heavy whipping cream, chilled

2 tablespoons confectioners' sugar

1 MAKE THE GRAHAM CRACKER CRUST Preheat the oven to 350°F. Place the steam rack in the bottom of the pressure cooker and add the water. Grease an 8-inch springform pan with cooking spray and wrap the bottom with foil to prevent the filling from leaking.

2 Combine all the ingredients for the crust in a large bowl and mix to combine. Press into the springform pan and up the sides. Bake until golden brown, 10 to 12 minutes. Remove from the oven and allow to cool completely.

continued

3 MAKE THE FILLING Whisk together the ingredients for the filling in a medium bowl and transfer to the springform pan. Smooth the top of the filling. Cover with foil and secure the bottom with the foil strap (see page 9). Place in the pressure cooker.

4 Secure the lid and set on Manual with high pressure for 15 minutes. Allow to naturally release for 10 minutes, then quick release and remove the lid. The center of the pie should jiggle slightly. If the pie still has a runny center, secure the lid again on the pressure cooker and select Manual with high pressure for another 4 minutes and check again.

5 Allow to cool to room temperature, then cover with plastic wrap and place in the refrigerator to set for 3 to 4 hours.

6 MAKE THE WHIPPED CREAM Whip the cream in a large bowl using a handheld mixer or in the bowl of a stand mixer fitted with a whisk attachment until soft peaks form, 3 to 4 minutes. Add the confectioners' sugar and continue whipping until soft-medium peaks form.

7 Remove the springform pan and garnish the pie with whipped cream.

BOURBON PECAN PIE

★ ★ ★

A holiday classic gets a Southern twist—a taste of bourbon. Try adding chocolate chips for an even richer flavor!

SERVES 4 TO 6
PREP TIME: 25 minutes
COOK TIME: 50 minutes
+ 1 hour to cool

FOR THE CRUST

1½ cups water

Cooking spray, for pan

1½ cups graham cracker crumbs

3 tablespoons unsalted butter, melted

1 tablespoon honey

½ teaspoon kosher salt

FOR THE FILLING

⅔ cup corn syrup

¼ cup dark brown sugar

2 tablespoons molasses

2 tablespoons bourbon (optional)

1 teaspoon vanilla extract

1 teaspoon kosher salt

3 large eggs

1¼ cups pecan halves

Whipped cream (pages 177–78 or store bought), to serve

1 **MAKE THE CRUST** Preheat the oven to 350°F. Place the steam rack in the bottom of the pressure cooker pot and add the water. Grease an 8-inch springform pan with cooking spray. Wrap the bottom of the pan with foil to prevent the filling from leaking.

2 Combine the graham cracker crumbs, butter, honey, and salt in a large bowl until the mixture just comes together. Transfer to the pan and press down to form a crust. Place in the oven and bake until golden brown, 10 to 12 minutes. Allow to cool completely.

3 **MAKE THE FILLING** Combine the corn syrup, brown sugar, molasses, bourbon, vanilla, salt, and eggs. Place the pecan

continued

halves on top of the crust. Pour the filling mixture over the nuts and cover with a paper towel and piece of foil. Make a foil strap (see page 9) around the base of the pan and place on the steam rack.

 Secure the lid and cook on Manual with high pressure for 28 minutes. Allow to naturally release, then remove the lid.

 Remove the pie and cool to room temperature. Serve with whipped cream.

BOURBON PECAN BREAD PUDDING

★ ★ ★

This classic dessert favorite gets a Southern twist with a splash of bourbon! It is the perfect dish for using leftover or stale bread. Add your favorite nuts or dried fruit to this dessert to mix it up.

SERVES 4 TO 6

PREP TIME: 25 minutes
COOK TIME: 25 minutes

————

SLOW COOKER
SETTING

Follow the method below, adding an additional ½ cup of milk to the mixture in step 2. For step 3, once the lid is secure, select the Slow Cook normal setting and cook for 2½ to 3 hours or until cooked through. Proceed with step 4.

1½ cups water

1 tablespoon unsalted butter, to grease, plus 3 tablespoons butter, melted

⅓ cup dark brown sugar

2 tablespoons honey

3 large eggs, beaten

½ cup low-fat milk

1 teaspoon kosher salt

1 teaspoon vanilla extract

½ teaspoon cinnamon

¼ teaspoon ground nutmeg

2 tablespoons bourbon

4 cups ½-inch-cubed day-old bread

½ cup pecans, roughly chopped

Vanilla ice cream or cold heavy cream and maple syrup, to serve

1 Place the steam rack inside of the pressure cooker and add the water. Grease a 6-inch round cake pan or soufflé dish with 1 tablespoon of butter.

2 Whisk together melted butter, brown sugar, honey, eggs, milk, salt, vanilla, cinnamon, nutmeg, and bourbon in a large bowl. Add the bread cubes and press down to submerge. Allow to soak for 15 minutes. Add the pecans, stir to combine, and transfer to the cake pan. Cover with a paper towel and a piece of foil and place on the steam rack in the pressure cooker.

3 Secure the lid and place on Manual with high pressure for 10 minutes. Allow to naturally release for 10 minutes, then quick release and remove the lid. Be sure that the center still jiggles slightly and that the egg is cooked through. If the center is still runny, secure the lid again on the pressure cooker and place on Manual with high pressure for another 4 minutes. Quick release, remove the lid, and check again.

4 If desired, preheat the oven to 400°F. Place the bread pudding in the oven to toast the top of the bread cubes, about 5 minutes. Remove and serve with vanilla ice cream or cold heavy cream and maple syrup.

PEACH AND BERRY COBBLER

★ ★ ★

Use your favorite fresh or frozen fruit in this dessert to create the taste of summer all year long. The pressure cooker allows you to cook this cobbler while you are eating dinner. Using a baking mix, such as Bisquick, keeps this dessert stress-free.

SERVES 4
PREP TIME: 10 minutes
COOK TIME: 22 minutes

SLOW COOKER
SETTING

Combine the filling ingredients and place the mixture into the bottom of the pressure cooker greased with cooking spray. Combine the topping ingredients and dollop the topping on the fruit. Secure the lid and place on the Slow Cook low setting for 3 hours or until set.

FOR THE FILLING

1 cup water

1 (15-ounce) bag frozen sliced peaches, thawed

1 (12-ounce) bag frozen berries, thawed

⅓ cup sugar

2 tablespoons honey

2 teaspoons cinnamon

3 tablespoons cornstarch

FOR THE TOPPING

2 cups baking mix, such as Bisquick

½ cup milk

½ teaspoon cinnamon

¼ cup sugar

½ cup old-fashioned oats

1 MAKE THE FILLING Place the steam rack in the bottom of the pressure cooker. Fill the bottom with the 1 cup of water.

2 Combine the fruit, sugar, honey, cinnamon, and cornstarch in a large bowl. Pour into four 4-ounce ramekins, a 6-inch soufflé dish, or a 6-inch round cake pan. Make a foil strap (see page 9) that can secure the bottom of the dish and act as a handle when placing into the pot.

3 MAKE THE TOPPING Combine all the ingredients for the biscuit topping in a medium bowl. Dollop the topping on top of the fruit.

4 Secure the lid and cook on Manual with high pressure for 10 minutes. Release using natural release.

5 Preheat the oven to broil. Place the soufflé dish under the broiler to toast until the oats are crisp and golden brown, 1 to 2 minutes. Remove and serve.

TROPICAL RICE PUDDING

★ ★ ★

Bring the beach to you with this pineapple-studded coconut-lime rice pudding. Add a dash of rum for a fun piña colada–inspired dessert. This pudding is delicious when warm, or you can chill it in the refrigerator before serving.

2 (15-ounce) cans full-fat coconut milk

½ cup milk

¼ cup dark brown sugar

2 tablespoons honey

1 cup Arborio rice

½ teaspoon kosher salt

½ teaspoon vanilla extract

1 egg, beaten

2 limes, zested and juiced

1 (8-ounce) can crushed pineapple, drained

1 teaspoon cinnamon

¾ cup sweetened coconut

1 Combine the coconut milk, milk, brown sugar, honey, rice, salt, and vanilla in the bowl of the pressure cooker.

2 Secure the lid and set on Manual with high pressure for 10 minutes. Allow to naturally release for 5 minutes, then quick release and remove the lid.

3 Add the egg, lime zest and juice, pineapple, cinnamon, and coconut, while stirring consistently. Remove the metal pot insert from the pressure cooker and allow the mixture to thicken and cool. Serve warm or cold.

SERVES 4 TO 6

PREP TIME: 5 minutes
COOK TIME: 20 minutes

SLOW COOKER SETTING

Follow the method below. For step 2, once the lid is secure, select the Slow Cook high setting and cook for 2½ to 3 hours or until the rice is cooked through. Remove the lid and stir in the egg, lime zest and juice, pineapple, cinnamon, and coconut. Serve warm or cold.

PEANUT SEA SALT BROWNIES

★ ★ ★

SERVES 4 TO 6
PREP TIME: 15 minutes
COOK TIME: 30 minutes

Yes! The chocolatey goodness of a brownie can be made in a pressure cooker. The classic combo of peanuts and chocolate with a hint of sea salt fulfills the salty-sweet desire everyone has in a dessert.

1½ cups water

Cooking spray, for greasing pan

4 tablespoons unsalted butter, softened

3 ounces bittersweet chocolate chips, divided

3 ounces semisweet chocolate chips, divided

⅔ cup all-purpose flour

½ teaspoon baking powder

½ teaspoon kosher salt

½ cup light brown sugar

2 large eggs

1 teaspoon vanilla

⅔ cup salted roasted peanuts

Flaky sea salt

1 Place the steam rack in the bottom of the pressure cooker and add the water. Grease a 7-inch round cake pan with cooking spray.

2 Heat a saucepan with 1 inch of water until simmering and place a glass bowl on top. Add 2 ounces of each chocolate to the bowl and stir until melted and smooth.

3 Whisk the flour, baking powder, and kosher salt together in a medium bowl. In a separate medium bowl, whisk the brown sugar, eggs, and vanilla until combined. While whisking, add the melted chocolate mixture to the sugar mixture and whisk until smooth. Add the flour mixture to the chocolate mixture and whisk until smooth. Stir in the roasted peanuts and remaining chocolate chips and pour into the cake pan. Sprinkle with sea salt, if desired. Cover with a piece of paper towel and then foil. Make a foil strap (see page 9) to secure the bottom of the pan and place in the pressure cooker.

4 Secure the lid and set on Manual with high pressure for 20 minutes. Allow to naturally release for 10 minutes, then quick release.

5 Remove the brownies from the pressure cooker and allow to cool to room temperature. Slice and serve.

STRAWBERRY SHORTCAKE COBBLER

★ ★ ★

This ultimate summer classic calls for strawberries, but you can use other favorite fresh berries for this dessert too. Using the zest and juice of your favorite citrus to the berries makes the flavors pop!

SERVES 4 TO 6

PREP TIME: 15 minutes
COOK TIME: 20 minutes

SLOW COOKER
SETTING

Place the filling mixture in the bottom of the slow cooker greased with cooking spray. Dollop with the topping, cover, and place on the Slow Cook low setting for 3 hours or until set.

FOR THE FILLING

1½ cups water

Cooking spray, to grease

3 cups strawberries, hulled and sliced

¼ cup sugar

1 lemon, zested and juiced

2 tablespoons cornstarch or arrowroot flour

FOR THE TOPPING

2 cups baking mix, such as Bisquick

¾ cup old-fashioned oats

½ cup milk

½ teaspoon cinnamon

¼ cup sugar

Whipped cream (pages 177–78 or store bought)

1 **MAKE THE FILLING** Place the steam rack in the pressure cooker and fill with the water. Grease a 6-inch soufflé dish or 6-inch round cake pan with cooking spray.

2 Combine the strawberries, sugar, lemon zest and juice, and cornstarch in a large bowl and transfer to the baking dish.

3 **MAKE THE TOPPING** Combine the baking mix, oats, milk, cinnamon, and sugar in a large bowl and dollop on top of the filling. Cover with a paper towel and then a piece of foil. Make a foil strap (see page 9) to secure the bottom of the pan, then place on top of the steam rack.

4 Secure the lid and place on Manual with high pressure for 10 minutes. Allow to naturally release for 10 minutes, then quick release and remove the lid.

5 Allow to cool for 5 minutes, then serve warm with whipped cream.

ACKNOWLEDGMENTS

★ ★ ★

First and foremost, thank you to everyone at The Countryman Press, especially Ann Treistman, Aurora Bell, and Devorah Backman—this book would be nowhere without your ideas, insight, and expertise. Thank you for your support and for allowing me to take my own creative direction. It is too fun working with you all!

Sharon Bowers, thank you for all of your guidance throughout this whole process and keeping every moment light. Your inspiration is woven throughout this book.

And, as always, thank you to my parents for your endless love and support, as well as your encouragement to keep me creative everyday. I hope you enjoy your recipe suggestions as much as I did.

INDEX

★ ★ ★

PHOTO CREDITS